BLAKE'S

Spelling Guide

for primary students

Del Merrick

PASCAL PRESS

Blake's Spelling Guide

Reprinted 2010 twice, 2011, 2012

ISBN: 978 1 92136 751 9

Published by Pascal Press
PO Box 250
Glebe NSW 2037
www.pascalpress.com.au
contact@pascalpress.com.au

Author: Del Merrick
Publisher: Lynn Dickinson
Edited by Shelley Barons & Kerry Davies
Design and illustration by Janice Bowles

Printed by Green Giant Press

CONTENTS

AUSTRALIAN CURRICULUM CORRELATIONS

LANGUAGE	ELABORATIONS	ACELA	PAGE
Expressing and developing ideas			
Know how to use onset and rime to spell words	★ breaking words into onset and rime, for example c/at ★ building word families using onset and rime, for example h/ot, g/ot, n/ot, sh/ot, sp/ot	1438	7 12
Know that regular one-syllable words are made up of letters and common letter clusters that correspond to the sounds heard, and how to use visual memory to write high-frequency words	★ writing one-syllable words containing known blends, for example 'bl', 'st' ★ learning an increasing number of high frequency sight words recognised in shared texts and in texts being read independently (for example 'one', 'have', 'them', 'about')	1778	16-17 39, 75 -76
Understand how to use digraphs, long vowels, blends and silent letters to spell words, and use morphemes and syllabification to break up simple words and use visual memory to write irregular words	★ drawing on knowledge of high frequency sight words ★ drawing on knowledge of sound–letter relationships (for example breaking words into syllables and phonemes) ★ using known words in writing and spell unknown words using developing visual, graphophonic and morphemic knowledge	1471	39-40, 75-76 35-36, 38 9-34, 41-44, 50-51, 53
Recognise common prefixes and suffixes and how they change a word's meaning	★ joining discussion about how a prefix or suffix affects meaning, for example uncomfortable, older, and division	1472	63-64, 83-89
Understand how to use sound–letter relationships and knowledge of spelling rules, compound words, prefixes, suffixes, morphemes and less common letter combinations, for example 'tion'	★ using spelling strategies such as: phonological knowledge (for example diphthongs and other ambiguous vowel sounds in more complex words); three-letter clusters (for example 'thr', 'shr', 'squ'); visual knowledge (for example more complex single syllable homophones such as 'break/brake', 'ate/eight'); morphemic knowledge (for example inflectional endings in single syllable words, plural and past tense); generalisations (for example to make a word plural when it ends in 's', 'sh', 'ch', or 'z' add 'es')	1485	19-32, 37, 41-44, 45-48, 50-52, 59-61, 78-79
Recognise high frequency sight words	★ becoming familiar with most high-frequency sight words	1486	39-40, 75-76
Understand how to use strategies for spelling words, including spelling rules, knowledge of morphemic word families, spelling generalisations, and letter combinations including double letters	★ using phonological knowledge (for example long vowel patterns in multi-syllabic words); consonant clusters (for example 'straight', 'throat', 'screen', 'squawk') ★ using visual knowledge (for example diphthongs in more complex words and other ambiguous vowel sounds, as in 'oy', 'oi', 'ou', 'ow', 'ould', 'u', 'ough', 'au', 'aw'); silent beginning consonant patterns (for example 'gn' and 'kn') ★ applying generalisations, for example doubling (for example 'running'); 'e'-drop (for example 'hoping')	1779	19-25, 29-32, 26-28, 34
Recognise homophones and know how to use context to identify correct spelling	★ using meaning and context when spelling words (for example when differentiating between homophones such as 'to', 'too', 'two'	1780	59-61, 78-79
Understand how to use banks of known words as well as word origins, prefixes,suffixes and morphemes to learn and spell new words	★ learning that many complex words were originally hyphenated but have become 'prefixed' as in 'uncommon', 'renew' 'email' and 'refine' ★ talking about how suffixes change over time and new forms are invented to reflect changing attitudes to gender, for example 'policewoman', 'salesperson'; 'air hostess'/'steward' or 'flight attendant	1513	58
Recognise uncommon plurals, for example'foci'	★ using knowledge of word origins and roots and related words to interpret and spell unfamiliar words, and learning about how these roots impact on plurals	1514	50-51, 70-71, 90-95
Understand how to use banks of known words, word origins, base words, suffixes and prefixes, morphemes, spelling patterns and generalisations to learn and spell new words, for example technical words and words adopted from other languages	★ adopting a range of spelling strategies to recall and attempt to spell new words ★ using a dictionary to correct students' own spelling	1526	40-42, 45-49, 68-69, 70-71, 72, 75-76, 82-95
Understand how to use spelling rules and word origins, for example Greek and Latin roots, base words, suffixes, prefixes, spelling patterns and generalisations to learn new words and how to spell them		1539	40-42, 45-49, 68-69, 70-71, 72, 75-76, 82-95

AUSTRALIAN CURRICULUM CORRELATIONS

LANGUAGE	ELABORATIONS	ACELA	PAGE
Sound and letter knowledge			
Recognise rhymes, syllables and sounds (phonemes) in spoken words	★ listening to the sounds a student hears in the word, and writing letters to represent those sounds ★ identifying rhyme and syllables in spoken words ★ identifying and manipulating sounds (phonemes) in spoken words ★ identifying onset and rime in one-syllable spoken words	1439	9-13, 15-18, 37, 68-69 5, 35-36
Recognise the letters of the alphabet and know there are lower and upper case letters	★ identifying familiar and recurring letters and the use of upper and lower case in written texts in the classroom and community ★ using familiar and common letters in handwritten and digital communications	1440	4-5,6 6
Manipulate sounds in spoken words including phoneme deletion and substitution	★ recognising words that start with a given sound, end with a given sound, have a given medial sound, rhyme with a given word ★ recognising and producing rhyming words ★ replacing sounds in spoken words (for example replace the 'm' in 'mat' with 'c' to form a new word 'cat') ★ saying sounds in order for a given spoken word (for example f/i/sh, th/i/s)	1457	9, 12, 17 98 9-11. 7, 37
Recognise sound-letter matches including common vowel and consonant digraphs and consonant blends	★ saying words with the same onset as a given word (for example words that begin like 'd/og', 'bl/ue') ★ saying words with the same rime as a given word (for example words that end like 'c/at', 'pl/ay')	1458	9-11, 13 12
Understand the variability of sound-letter matches	★ recognising that letters can have more than one sound (for example 'u' in 'cut', 'put', 'use' and a in 'cat', 'father', 'any') ★ recognising sounds that can be produced by different letters (for example the /s/ sound in 'sat', 'cent', 'scene')	1459	5,15 5, 9-10, 13-14
Recognise most sound–letter matches including silent letters, vowel/consonant digraphs and many less common sound–letter combinations	★ recognising when some letters are silent, for example knife, listen, castle, and providing the sound for less common sound-letter matches, for example 'tion'	1474	9-18, 64, 86-88
LITERACY		**ACELY**	
Creating Texts			
Reread and edit text for spelling,	★ checking spelling using a dictionary ★ using glossaries, print and digital dictionaries and spell check to edit spelling, realising that spell check accuracy depends on understanding the word function, for example there/their; rain/reign	1672 1685	67 67, 70-71, 78-79, 96-98

HOW TO USE THIS BOOK

Blake's Spelling Guide will provide you with the tools you need to be a successful speller. It will help you gain knowledge about the use of the alphabet and to develop concepts about manipulating words to fit their context.

This guide contains:

- sections on each key element for developing good spelling skills
- lots of examples for each new concept
- plenty of opportunities to practise using the TRY THIS tests
- a GLOSSARY with concise definitions for all the major terms (includes examples)
- twelve very useful WORD LISTS covering everything from Homonyms and Antonyms to Frequently Misspelt Words and Latin and Greek roots.

This guide is a vital reference for everyone wanting to be a great speller.

ABOUT THE AUTHOR

Del Merrick is an experienced teacher currently working for Education Queensland as a Support Teacher, Learning Difficulties. She has taught in many primary schools, both nationally and internationally, and has undertaken various educator positions including Key Teacher, English; Further Literacy In-service Project Consultant; 'First Steps' Tutor; Education Adviser; Literacy and Key Learning Area Regional Coordinator, English.

Del has worked extensively with educators in both the state and non-state systems, providing strong leadership and professional expertise while guiding and supporting changed classroom methodology and improved literacy practices. She is the author of many educational materials, including the best-selling *Targeting Grammar* series, and has designed an extensive range of professional development workshops and resource materials for educators. Her personal interests include a passion for poetry and music.

THE ENGLISH LANGUAGE

The English language has evolved over many centuries. It had its beginnings in the spoken languages of the primitive peoples scattered throughout the villages of England, Scotland and Wales.

Words are constantly being added or discarded

During its long journey, the English language gathered hundreds of words from the traders and invaders who came to its shores. Explorers brought back new products and plants, each with its own words and unique pronunciation and spelling. The advent of the Industrial Revolution brought new machines for manufacturing and led to the rapid growth of factories, employment and city living.

The English language continues to respond and adapt to a changing world, as new inventions and technologies create a need for new words. Words are constantly being added, or discarded, as lifestyles change and countries develop culturally, socially and economically. Recent additions include Googling, texting, downloading and surfing the net.

The first person to standardise the spelling of many English words was William Caxton, who invented the first printing press over five hundred years ago.

As a language, English has a relatively simple grammar and avoids some of the complex demands of other languages. For example, German requires the use of seven different words for the English word you. In English there are two articles, a and the. In French, writers must choose between le for masculine nouns and la for feminine nouns. In English, common nouns are neither masculine nor feminine.

English is spoken by millions of people across the world to communicate with each other. It is the global language of business, science, politics, education, tourism and the pop music industry.

Many people who can speak in English cannot write it. Writing demands the knowledge of how to form words by using symbols that represent speech sounds. This is the essence of spelling. If people are to communicate with each other effectively and without ambiguity, an agreed system of spelling is needed.

A B C D E F G
H I J K L M N
O P Q R S T U
V W X Y Z

a b c d e f g
h i j k l m n o
p q r s t u v
w x y z

English spelling is based on the Latin alphabet — a series of symbols which had their origins in ancient Egypt. These symbols changed over the years, influenced first by the Greeks and later by the Romans, to finally become the 26 letters of the alphabet that we use today.

THE LANGUAGE OF SPELLING

Consonants are limited in the sounds they represent. Most consonants only have one sound. Doubled consonants also have only one sound. For example, egg, add, off, butter and kiss.

Some consonants work in pairs to represent one sound. These are called consonant digraphs. These consonant 'buddies' are ch, sh, th, ph and wh.

Some consonant sounds slide into each other, especially at the beginnings of words. These are called consonant blends. For example: frog and plum.

The **vowels** are very busy letters. They do a lot of work. On their own they can represent a number of different speech sounds. For example, the letter **a** represents a different sound in each of these words – hat, hate, path, water, what, about. Combined with other vowels or consonants, they represent a wider range of speech sounds. These are called vowel digraphs or vowel teams. For example the ai in rain or the ea in tea.

Letters are put together to form words. For example cat, football and chocolate. Many of these letters are put together in patterns and recur in many words. For example, pet occurs in petrol, carpet, petulant, petunia and repetitive.

Every word contains one or more syllables. For example, book has one syllable, soccer has two, banana has three and antidisestablishmentarianism has an amazing eleven syllables!

The alphabet contains 26 letters.

Each letter has a name.

Each letter represents a speech sound.

Consonants
b c d f g h j
k l m n p q r s
t v w x y z

Vowels
a e i o u

THE ALPHABET

The alphabet has 26 letters.

a b c d e f g h i j k l m n
o p q r s t u v w x y z

Vowels

a e i o u

Short vowels have a short snappy sound:
bag beg big bog bug

Long vowels say their name:
cake these ride
home tube

Vowels can work in teams:
ai ea ee ie oa oo
rain tea sheep
pie boat moon

Consonants

With 1 sound

b d f h j k l m
n p q r s t
v w x y z

Some consonants slide together – these are consonant blends

bl br cl cr dr dw fl
fr gl gr pl pr sn sl st
str sm sn sp spl spr
sq sk sc scr tr tw

Some consonants are buddies with only 1 sound

ch ph
sh th wh

With 2 sounds

c and g

The letter 'y' sometimes takes the place of a vowel sound: sunny, gym, cyclone.

WHAT WE NEED TO KNOW ABOUT SPELLING

1 We need to know we can write many words exactly as we **sound** them.

c + a + t = cat

p + i + g = pig

con + tent = content

To remember these words, we say them with our mouth and listen to the chunks of sound with our **ears**.

2 We need to recognise many words with our **eyes** because they don't follow a sound pattern.

done, not dun

who, not hoo

was, not woz

To remember these words, we **look** at them and then close our eyes and picture them in our mind; then we write them from that memory.

What We Need to Know About Spelling

3 We need to know how to **add endings** to some words, so that the words we write make sense. For example:

I wash my face.
I am washing my face.
I have washed my face.

I have a toy car.
Bill has three toy cars.

Jo is a slow runner.
He runs slowly.

To remember these words, we need to know the **common endings** and some **rules** for using them.

4 We need to know that whole families of words have grown from their **Latin and Greek roots**, like a family tree. Studying these roots helps us to remember many words.

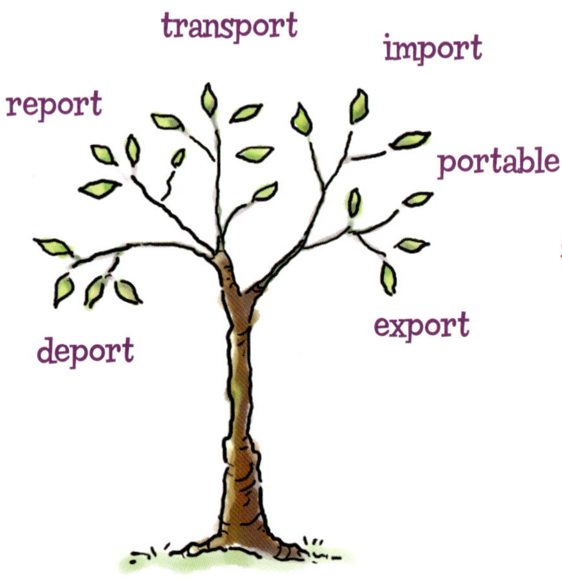

porto – I carry

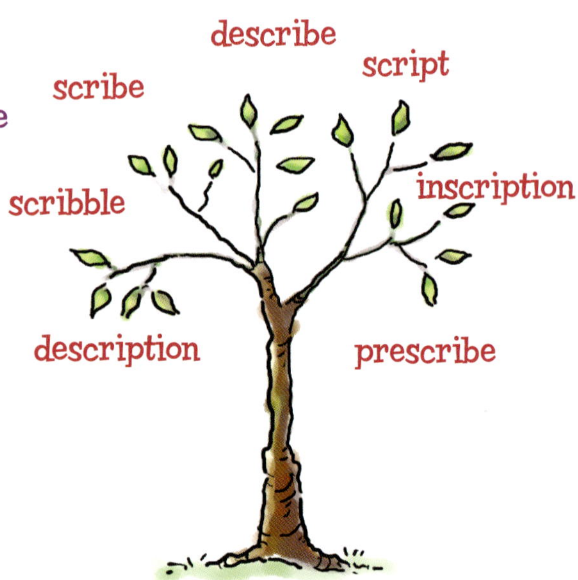

scribo – I write

CONSONANTS

b c d f g h j k l m n
p q r s t v w x y z

There are 21 consonants in the English alphabet.

Most consonants represent only one speech sound, especially at the beginning of a word.

b is the first sound in 

f is the first sound in 

s is the last sound in 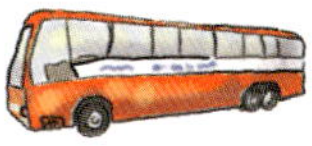

Write a consonant under each picture to represent the first sound you hear in the word.

________ ________ ________

The letter q is ALWAYS followed by u: queen, quit

Write a consonant under each picture to represent the last sound you hear in the word.

________ ________ ________

Put in the missing consonants to complete this nursery rhyme.

Jack and _ill went u_ the hi_ _
To _etch a pai_ of _ater.
Jack fell _own and bro_e his crow_
An_ Jill came _umbling af_er.

TRY THIS

CONSONANTS WITH TWO SOUNDS

The consonants **c** and **g** each represent two different sounds.

Letter **c** followed by an **a, o** or **u** is a 'hard' sound like the **k** in kite.

eg cat, coat, coffee, cup

Letter **c** followed by an **e, i** or **y** is a 'soft' sound like the **s** in sun.

eg cent, city, face, cyclone, Nancy

Say these words. Is the c soft or hard?

can, circle, icy, picnic, raced, corn,

cosy, dancer, fancy, camp, cycle, circus

Letter **g** is sometimes a 'hard' sound like the **g** in girl.

eg get, dog, gum, game, mug

Letter **g** is sometimes a 'soft' sound like the **j** in jeans.

eg gentle, giant, gym, page, edgy

Say these words. Is the g soft or hard?

goal, gorgeous, stage, angel, garden, mongrel

bridge, bagel, spongy, manager, gate, large

The letter **r** at the beginning of a word has a different sound to one at the end. Compare the beginning and end sounds of these words: rider, radiator, rotor and remember.

Here the **r** at the end works with the vowel before it to form a different sound called a **schwa** sound. The schwa sound often occurs in **unstressed syllables**.

INITIAL CONSONANT BLENDS

Words are formed by placing letters in a particular order or sequence.
A word can begin with any **vowel**, eg apple, egg, in, orange and up.
A word can begin with any **consonant**,
eg box, house, man, kite, zoo.

All initial consonants can be followed by a vowel,
eg wag pet win pot hug

Only some consonants can be followed by another consonant.
When we say these two sounds, we slide them together to make a blended sound.

These words begin with a **consonant blend**:
black drop spot frog twin play stop

Consonant Blends

b	bl br
c	cl cr
f	fl fr
g	gl gr
p	pl pr
d	dr dw
t	tr tw
s	sc sk sl sm sn sp sq(u)
	st sw scr spl spr str

l and r are most often used in blended consonants.

TRY THIS

Add a consonant to complete these words.
My b _ other and I went to Melbourne by p _ ane. We f _ ew high above the c _ ouds.
The sun was shining in the b _ ue s _ y.
We arrived at th _ ee o'clock. Our f _ iend, T _ ent, met us and d _ ove us into the city. We would s _ay with him for t _ elve days.

FINAL CONSONANT BLENDS

A consonant blend at the end of a word always follows a vowel.
The vowel and the consonant blend form a letter string.

camp bend pink old must

These letter strings appear in many words, which we call rhyming words. So, if we can spell one word, we can also spell many words like it.

Add the missing letters and say the words.

camp	bend	pink	gold	must
damp	lend	sink	cold	rust
lamp	send	link	fold	dust
r	m	w	h	cr
st	tr	dr	s	tr

Write some rhyming words with these letter strings.

-est	-ing	-ent	-ump	-and

How many words can you make?

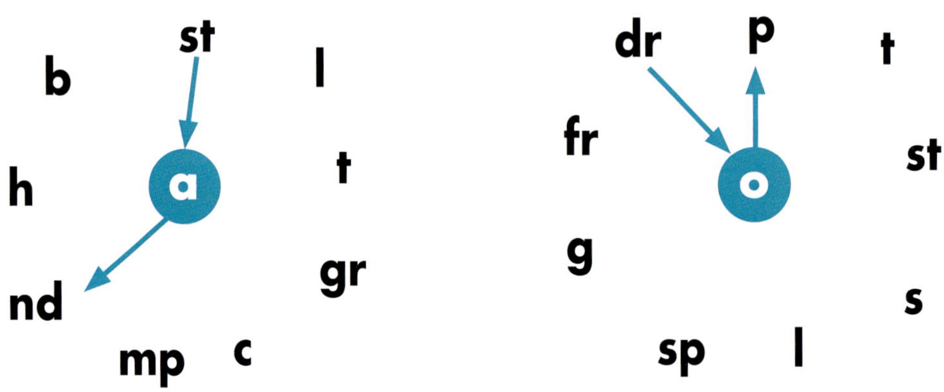

CONSONANT BUDDIES

Sometimes, two consonants together represent **one** speech sound.

shop chop Christmas they think phone why duck

These consonant buddies can appear in different parts of a word.

	at the beginning	in the middle	on the end
sh	ship	cushion	push
ch	chop	Richard	pinch
ch	choir	anchor	ache
th *(voiced)*	them	mother	bathe
th *(unvoiced)*	thing	nothing	month
ph	phone	nephew	graph
wh	what	nowhere	–

A common letter string is a vowel followed by **tch**. For example:
catch snatch fetch stretch pitch stitch hutch crutch

The consonant buddies **ck** can only be used at the end of a syllable, and only after a 'short' vowel. Think of them as the 'kissing cousins'.
For example:
duck pack lock peck stick tackle rocket wicked

Circle the consonant buddies in this text.

The champ stepped up to bat. There was a hush as the pitcher checked his line and length.
With a quick flick of his arm, he pitched the ball.
There was a loud crack as the champ hit the ball.
The players on the bench cheered when no one was able to catch the ball. With that ball the match was won!

SILENT LETTERS

In some words, certain consonants are not pronounced.

These are often called **silent letters**.

k in know and knife
w in write and wring
g in gnaw and gnome
b in lamb and climb
l in walk and calm
n in autumn and hymn
t in listen and castle
gh in high and night

Here are some everyday words with **silent letters** in them.

kn	wr	gn	mb / bt
knee	wrap	gnat	bomb
knew	wreck	gnaw	climb
knight	wrestle	gnome	comb
knit	wriggle	campaign	crumb
knob	wring	design	lamb
knock	wrinkle	reign	numb
knot	wrist	resign	thumb
know	write	sign	
knowledge	wrong		debt
knuckle	wrote		doubt
l	**mn**	**st**	**gh**
calf	autumn	bustle	bought
calm	column	castle	caught
chalk	condemn	fasten	eight
could	hymn	glisten	freight
folk	solemn	listen	high
half		nestle	light
palm		rustle	night
talk		thistle	sigh
walk		whistle	thought
yolk		wrestle	weight

VOWELS

There are five vowels in the English alphabet.

a e i o u

There is always at least ONE vowel in a word.

I, be, cat, letter, banana

y sometimes does the work of a vowel:
by gym crazy cyclone style

TRY THIS

How many vowels are in this text?

Lulu was a fairy. She lived serenely in Bobby Sox's garden. She spent her days sitting on a swing under the frangipani tree.
She could see her beautiful reflection in the fishpond below. Two white ducks kept her quiet company. Peter and Bobby Sox always stopped for a chat as they went to and fro, on their way from here and there, and nowhere in particular.

There are:

☐ **a** vowels

☐ **e** vowels

☐ **i** vowels

☐ **o** vowels

☐ **u** vowels

The vowels represent a range of different speech sounds.

- They can have a short, snappy sound as in cat, pet, sit, pot and cup. *(See Short Vowels, p. 16.)*
- They can have a long, drawn-out sound as in cake, these, five, home and cube. *(See Long Vowels, p. 18)*
- They can work with each other in pairs, as in rain, sheep, tea, boat, pie, point, mouse and moon. *(See Vowel Teams, pp. 19–33.)*
- They can work with other consonants, as in day, for, cow, her, car and claws. *(See Vowel Teams, pp. 19–33.)*

SHORT VOWELS

Each vowel represents a short, snappy sound.
This is the first sound you hear in:

apple egg ink orange up

TRY THIS

Name the pictures below. Listen carefully for the sound represented by the vowel in the middle of each word. Write the words in the correct columns.

a	e	i	o	u

MORE ABOUT SHORT VOWELS

Short vowels are most often sandwiched between consonants. Knowing the short vowel sounds can help you spell many short words.

Write words to label the pictures.

r__t

t__p

b__x

l__d

tr__ck

p__g

j__g

n__st

d__g

cl__ck

t__nt

g__ft

d__ck

fl__g

n__t

Some of the short vowels have been left out of this extract from *Little Red Riding Hood*. Can you put them back?

Little Red Riding Hood's mother p _ cked a basket with _ ggs, b _ tter, bread and j _ m for Gr _ndma. Grandma l_ved in a c _ ttage in the m _ ddle of the wood. Little Red Riding Hood put on her r _ d cape and p _ cked up the basket. 'Do n _ t go _ ff the path,' said her mother as Little Red Riding Hood l _ ft the house. But she d _ d! She l _ ft the path to p _ ck flowers for her Grandma.

LONG VOWELS

Each vowel represents a long, drawn-out sound.

The sound of the vowel is the same as its name:

cake these ride home tube

We often make a short vowel into a long vowel by placing an e at the end.
The e is not sounded and is often called silent e.

For example:

hat	bit	rid
hate	bite	ride

TRY THIS

Name the pictures

_____e

_____e

_____e

_____e

_____e

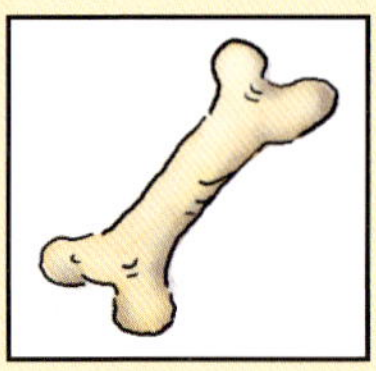

_____e

_____e

_____e

_____e

_____e

_____e

_____e

_____e

_____e

_____e

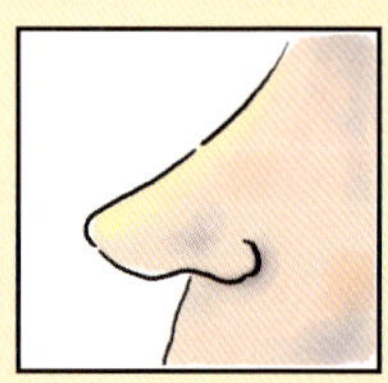

_____e

VOWEL TEAMS

Vowels can work with each other in pairs, or with other consonants, to represent different speech sounds.

These are called vowel digraphs or teams:

rain feet boat moon cloud saw car cow

Vowel teams representing the long a sound.

ai	ay	ei

train	**hay**	**eight**

TRY THIS

Add the vowel teams to spell these words:

chain	day	rein
p _ _ n	s _ _	v _ _ n
p _ _ nt	w _ _	v _ _ l
gr _ _ n	l _ _	_ _ ght
m _ _ l	p _ _	_ _ ghty
t _ _ l	pl _ _	w _ _ gh
l _ _ d	pr _ _	w _ _ ght
w _ _ t	cl _ _	fr _ _ ght
_ _ m	str _ _	sl _ _ gh
pr _ _ se	spr _ _	n _ _ gh

The gh is silent in these words.

- **ai** appears within a word.
- **ay** appears at the end of a word.
- Most plural nouns are formed by adding **s**.
- Present tense verbs are formed by adding **ing** but: drop the **e** before adding **ing** (praise, praising).
- Past tense verbs are formed by adding **ed** (exception: say, said).

How do you know whether a word contains ee or ea? It will LOOK right.

Vowel teams representing the long e sound.

ee	ea

sheep	leaves

TRY THIS

Add the vowel teams to spell these words:

deep	meat
t _ _th	n _ _ t
f _ _ d	b _ _ ch
w _ _ d	b _ _ d
f _ _ l	l _ _ f
st _ _ l	_ _ st
gr _ _ n	f _ _ st
b _ _ n	b _ _ k
sh _ _ t	gr _ _ se

- Add **es** to form the plural of nouns ending in **sh** or **ch** (beach, beaches; leash, leashes).
- To form the plural of nouns ending in **f**, change the **f** to **v** and add **es** (leaf, leaves). (Exception: roof, roofs)
- Add **s** to form most other plural nouns (exceptions: tooth, teeth; foot, feet; goose, geese).
- Present tense verbs are formed by adding **ing** (weed, weeding).
- Past tense verbs are formed by adding **ed** (weed, weeded) (some exceptions: feed, fed; eat, ate; read, read; freeze, froze; steal, stole; sleep, slept; speak, spoke; speed, sped; see, saw; seek, sought).
- If a word ends in **e**, drop the **e** before adding an ending beginning with a vowel (freeze, freezing – grease, greasy).
- Change the **y** to **i** then add an ending (greedy, greedily, greediness).

Vowel teams representing the long o sound.

oa	ow
 goat	 snow

Add the vowel teams to spell these words:

boat	flow
fl _ _ t	bl _ _
c _ _ t	gr _ _
c _ _ ch	sh _ _
l _ _ f	l _ _
l _ _ the	m _ _
s _ _ p	r _ _
c _ _ st	thr _ _
r _ _ st	yell _ _
thr _ _ t	foll _ _

Sometimes this sound is represented by oe
toe, hoe, doe

- Add **es** to form the plural of nouns ending in **ch** (coach, coaches).
- To form the plural of nouns ending in **f**, change the **f** to **v** and add **es** (loaf, loaves).
- Add **s** to form all other plural nouns.
- Present tense verbs are formed by adding **ing** (float, floating).
- Past tense verbs are formed by adding **ed** (float, floated).
- If a word ends in **e**, drop the **e** before adding an ending beginning with a vowel (loathe, loathing).
- Change the **y** to **i** before adding an ending (throaty, throatily, throatiness).

The vowel team oo represents two different speech sounds.

oo	oo
 moon	 books

Add vowel teams to spell these words:

spoon	hook
ball _ _ n	sh _ _ k
f _ _ d	l _ _ k
m _ _ d	t _ _ k
b _ _ t	f _ _ t
t _ _ th	w _ _ l
r _ _ m	st _ _ d
r _ _ f	h _ _ d
g _ _ se	g _ _ d
l _ _ se	w _ _ d

- Plural nouns are formed by adding **s**. There are some irregular plural nouns: tooth, teeth; foot, feet; goose, geese.
- Present tense verbs are formed by adding **ing** (cook, cooking).
- Past tense verbs are formed by adding **ed** (cook, cooked). Some past tense verbs are irregular (stand, stood; shake, shook; take, took).
- If a word ends in **e**, keep the **e** before adding an ending beginning with a consonant (loose, loosely).
- Change the **y** to **i** before adding an ending (gloomy, gloomily, gloominess).

The long i sound on the end of a word is usually represented by y:
by, my, cry

Add y and say these words:

dr _	cr _	tr _	sk _
fl _	sl _	pr _	sl _
fr _	st _	spr _	sh _

- Present tense verbs are formed by adding **ing** (dry, drying; fly, flying)
- Change the **y** to **i** before adding an ending when writing:
  - third-person present tense (cry, cries; dry, dries)
  - past participles (cry, cried; dry, dried)
  - noun plurals (sky, skies; fly, flies).
- Some past tense verbs are irregular (fly, flew).

Here is a table to help you.

Base verb	Third person present tense	Present participle	Past participle
dry	dries	drying	dried
fry	fries	frying	fried
cry	cries	crying	cried
spy	spies	spying	spied
try	tries	trying	tried
fly	flies	flying	flew

The **long i** sound can also be represented by **igh**. The **gh** is silent in these words, so you need to remember what these words look like when you spell them. Here is a list of words with this pattern.

high	tight	fight	right	night
sigh	light	flight	bright	knight
sight	might	fright	bight	slight

- Plural nouns are formed by adding **s** (light, lights).
- Present tense verbs are formed by adding **ing** (fight, fighting; sigh, sighing).
- Past tense verbs are formed by adding **ed** (sigh, sighed) .
- Some are irregular (fight, fought; light, lit).

The vowel team ie represents two different speech sounds.

ie	ie
 pie	 field

Add vowel teams to spell these words:

tie	piece
l _ _	n _ _ ce
d _ _	th _ _f
v _ _	ch _ _ f
p _ _ s	pr _ _ st
	bel _ _ ve
	bel _ _ f
	rel _ _ ve
	rel _ _ f
	gr _ _ f

- Plural nouns are formed by adding **s** (pie, pies; niece, nieces; belief, beliefs). NOTE: The plural of thief is thieves, but the plural of chief is chiefs.
- Change **f** to **v** when changing nouns to verbs and add **e**: (thief, thieve; belief, believe; relief, relieve; grief, grieve).
- Present tense verbs are formed by adding **ing**, but: drop the **e** before adding **ing** (pierce, piercing)
- Change the **ie** to **y** before adding **ing** (tie, tying; die, dying; lie, lying).
- Past tense verbs are formed by adding **ed** (field, fielded). For words that already end in **e**, you will just need to add the **d** (tie, tied; die, died; pierce, pierced; believe, believed).

The long u sound is represented by ue or ew.

ue	ew
	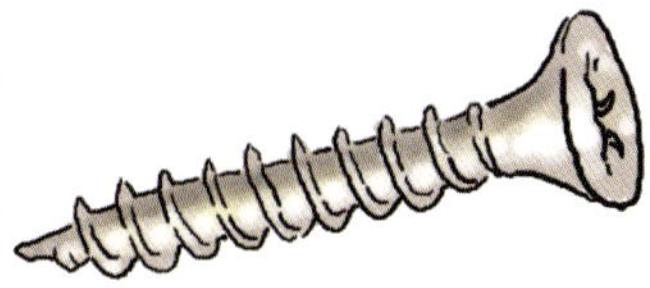
glue	screw

Add vowel teams to spell these words:

blue	blew
tr _ _	ch _ _
fl _ _	gr _ _
aven _ _	n _ _
reven_ _	kn _ _
stat _ _	st _ _
	fl _ _
	dr _ _
	f _ _
	j _ _ el

- Plural nouns are formed by adding **s** (screw, screws; statue, statues
- Present tense verbs are formed by adding **ing** (chew, chewing).
- Past tense verbs are formed by adding **ed** (stew, stewed). Some past tense verbs are irregular (draw, drew; fly, flew; blow, blew; know, knew; grow, grew).

The vowel teams au and aw represent the same speech sound.

au	aw
	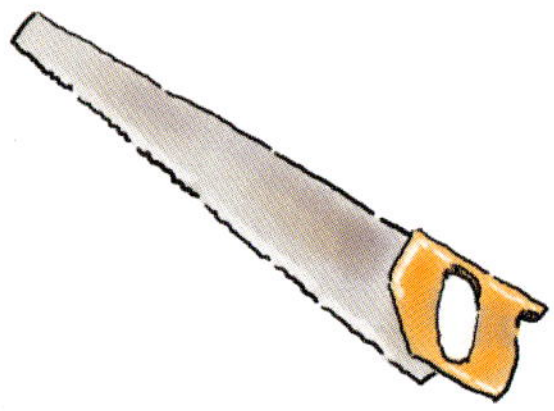
autumn	**saw**

TRY THIS

Add vowel teams to spell these words:

sauce	paw
t _ _ ght	j _ _
c _ _ ght	l _ _
n _ _ ghty	cl _ _
d _ _ ghter	dr _ _
p _ _ se	str _ _
c _ _ se	d _ _ n
l _ _ nch	l _ _ n
h _ _ nt	cr _ _ l
h _ _ l	sh _ _ l

The gh in caught, taught, naughty and daughter are silent letters.

- Plural nouns are formed by adding **s** (paw, paws; sauce, sauces).
- Add **es** to form the plural of nouns ending in **ch** (launch, launches).
- Present tense verbs are formed by adding **ing** (claw, clawing).
- Drop the **e** before adding **ing** (cause, causing; pause, pausing).
- Past tense verbs are formed by adding **ed** (claw, clawed; launch, launched). (Some are irregular draw, drew; see, saw).
- Change the **y** to **i** before adding an ending (saucy, saucily, sauciness; naughty, naughtily, naughtiness).

The vowel teams ou and ow represent the same speech sound.

ou	ow
 cloud	 cow

TRY THIS

Add the vowel teams to spell these words:

loud	how
b _ _ nce	n _ _
sh _ _ t	br _ _ n
d _ _ bt	cl _ _ n
h _ _ se	cr _ _ d
s _ _ nd	pr _ _ l
r _ _ nd	gr _ _ l
p _ _ ch	fl _ _ er
m _ _ th	sh _ _ er
pl _ _ gh	p _ _ der

The b in doubt and the gh in plough are silent letters.

- Plural nouns are formed by adding **s** (sound, sounds; crowd, crowds).
- Add **es** to form the plural of nouns ending in **ch** (pouch, pouches).
- Present tense verbs are formed by adding **ing** (shout, shouting; growl, growling).
- Drop the **e** before adding **ing** or **y** (bounce, bouncing, bouncy; browse, browsing; drowse, drowsy).
- Keep the **e** before adding an ending beginning with a consonant (announce, announcement; house, household).
- Past tense verbs are formed by adding **ed** (plough, ploughed; prowl, prowled).
- Change the **y** to **i** before adding an ending (drowsy, drowsily, drowsiness; cloudy, cloudiness).

The vowel teams oi and oy represent the same speech sound.

oi	oy

coins	toy

TRY THIS

Add vowel teams to spell these words:

oil	boy
b _ _ l	c _ _
f _ _ l	j _ _
sp _ _ l	enj _ _
j _ _ n	empl _ _
m _ _ st	destr _ _
v _ _ ce	ann _ _
p _ _ nt	r _ _ al
j _ _ nt	l _ _ al
n _ _ se	_ _ ster

- Plural nouns are formed by adding **s** (voice, voices; boy, boys).
- Present tense verbs are formed by adding **ing** (point, pointing; enjoy, enjoying).
- Drop the **e** before adding **ing** and **y** (voice, voicing; noise, noisy).
- Past tense verbs are formed by adding **ed** (join, joined; employ, employed).
- Change the **y** to **i** before adding an ending (noisy, noisily, noisiness).

The vowel teams air and are represent the same speech sound.

air	are

pair	square

Add vowel teams to spell these words:

air	bare
h _ _ _	c _ _ _
l _ _ _	r _ _ _
ch _ _ _	st _ _ _
f _ _ _	fl _ _ _
fl _ _ _	gl _ _ _
st _ _ _ s	sh _ _ _
f _ _ _ y	sn _ _ _
d _ _ _ y	sp _ _ _
rep _ _ _	prep _ _ _

- Plural nouns are formed by adding **s** (chair, chairs; flare, flares).
- Change the **y** to **i** before adding **es** (fairy, fairies).
- Present tense verbs are formed by adding **ing** (air, airing; repair, repairing).
- Drop the **e** before adding **ing** and **y** (stare, staring; glare, glary).
- Keep the **e** before adding an ending beginning with a consonant (care, careless; rare, rarely).
- Past tense verbs are formed by adding **ed** (air, aired; share, shared).

Here are two more ea teams – one has a short e sound, and one is controlled by r.

ea	ear
	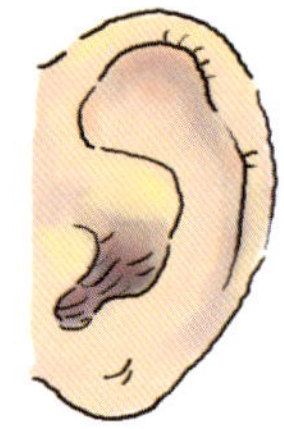
bread	ear

Add vowel teams to spell these words:

head	hear
h _ _ lth	d _ _ _
l _ _ d	y _ _ _
l _ _ ther	f _ _ _
f _ _ ther	cl _ _ _
spr _ _ d	sp _ _ _
d _ _ d	g _ _ _
d _ _ th	r _ _ _
d _ _ f	n _ _ _
br _ _ th	b _ _ _ d

- Plural nouns are formed by adding **s** (head, heads; year, years)
- Present tense verbs are formed by adding **ing** (spread, spreading; hear, hearing).
- Keep the **e** before adding an ending beginning with a consonant (measure, measurement).
- Past tense verbs are formed by adding **ed** (dread, dreaded; fear, feared).
  Exceptions: deal, dealt; read, read; lead, led; die, dead; swear, swore; wear, wore; hear, heard.
- Change the **y** to **i** before adding an ending (healthy, healthier; ready, readily, readiness; weary, wearily, weariness).

The vowels followed by r represent three different sounds.

ar

car

ar	or
far, park	for, pork

er	ir	ur
her	girl	turn

Add vowel teams to spell these words:

star	farm/er
j _ _	g _ _ /den
c _ _ d	p _ _ /cel
_ _ my	p _ _ t/ner
c _ _ ve	p _ _ /don
l _ _ ge	h _ _ /vest
m _ _ ch	cal/end/_ _
h _ _ sh	g _ _ /ment
sn _ _ l	_ _ /gu/ment
h _ _ m	_ _ t/ist

- Plural nouns are formed by adding **s** (star, stars; farm, farms).
- Add **es** to form the plural of nouns ending in **ch** or **sh** (arch, arches; marsh, marshes).
- Change **f** to **v** before adding **es** (scarf, scarves).
- Change the **y** to **i** before adding **es** (harmony, harmonies).
- Present tense verbs are formed by adding **ing** (cart, carting; park, parking): drop the **e** before adding **ing** (carve, carving; argue, arguing).
- Past tense verbs are formed by adding **ed** (start, started; march, marched).
- If a word ends in **ar**, double the **r** before adding an ending (star, starry; jar, jarring; char, charred).

Vowel teams or and oar share the same speech sound.
If the word ends in the or sound, a silent e is added.

or	ore	oar
		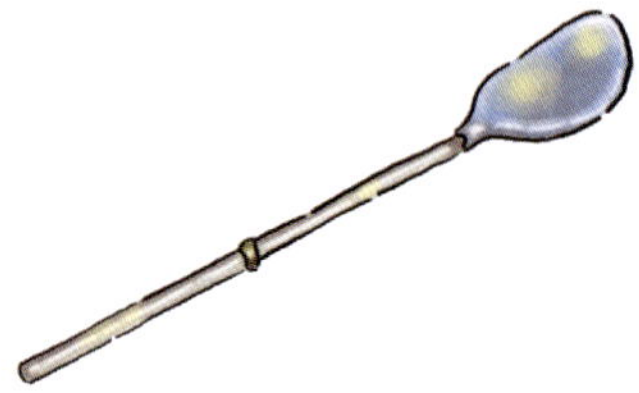
corn	core	oar

Add the vowel teams to spell these words:

horn	more	roar
b _ _ n	t _ _ _	s _ _ _
h _ _ se	b _ _ _	b _ _ _
f _ _ k	w _ _ _	h _ _ _ d
p _ _ k	p _ _ _	b _ _ _ d
l _ _ d	s _ _ _	ab _ _ _ d
c _ _ d	st _ _ _	c _ _ _ se
sh _ _ t	sn _ _ _	
sn _ _ t	sh _ _ _	
sn _ _ k/el	sw _ _ _	

- Plural nouns are formed by adding **s** (cord, cords; sore, sores).
- Present tense verbs are formed by adding ing (snort, snorting; board, boarding) drop the **e** before adding **ing** (store, storing; bore, boring).
- Past tense verbs are formed by adding **ed** (score, scored; roar, roared.
- Some are irregular (tear, tore; wear, wore).
- Drop the **e** before adding an ending beginning with a vowel (ignore, ignorant).
- Keep the **e** before adding an ending beginning with a consonant (sore, soreness; force, forceful).

Vowel teams er, ir and ur share the same speech sound.

er on the end of a word is usually a schwa sound – not stressed.
This sound is sometimes written as **or** (work, worm, word)
and **ear** (earth, earn, early).

er	**er** (schwa)	**ir**	**ur**
 **person**	 **rider**	 **girl**	 **burn**

TRY THIS

Add vowel teams to spell these words:

her	**baker**	**skirt**	**turn**
h _ _ d	butch _ _	sh _ _ t	ch _ _ ch
st _ _ n	danc _ _	d _ _ t	t _ _ tle
f _ _	teach _ _	st _ _	f _ _
p _ _ ch	sing _ _	b _ _ d	n _ _ se
s _ _ ve	skat _ _	f _ _ st	p _ _ se
n _ _ ve	rul _ _	th _ _ d	s _ _ f
j _ _ k	rubb _ _	th _ _ st	sp _ _ t

- Plural nouns are formed by adding **s** (herd, herds; dancer, dancers; bird, birds; purse, purses).
- Add **es** to form the plural of nouns ending in **ch** or **sh** (church churches).
- Present tense verbs are formed by adding **ing** (perch, perching; surf, surfing).
  drop the **e** before adding **ing** (nurse, nursing; serve, serving).
- Past tense verbs are formed by adding **ed** (jerk, jerked; turn, turned).
- Drop the **e** before adding an ending beginning with a vowel (nerve, nervous; serve, servant).
- Keep the **e** before adding an ending beginning with a consonant (furtive, furtively).

VISUAL PATTERNS

Some words have letter strings that make a pattern you can see rather than hear.

They look the same, but they are not always pronounced in the same way.

rough, cough, drought, though, bought

ough

trough

Add vowel teams to spell these words:

rough	sought
t _ _ _ _	th _ _ _ _ t
en _ _ _ _	b _ _ _ _ t
c _ _ _ _	n _ _ _ _ t
tr _ _ _ _	dr _ _ _ _ t
	br _ _ _ t

- Plural nouns are formed by adding **s** (drought, droughts; trough, troughs).
- Present tense verbs are formed by adding **ing** (cough, coughing).
- Past tense verbs are formed by adding **ed** (cough, coughed). Some words are already in past tense — bought; brought; thought; sought; fought.

SYLLABLES

Words are made up of 'chunks' of sound called syllables. Every syllable contains a vowel sound.

Every syllable contains a vowel sound.

Generally, the words we use every day have between one and five syllables.

For example:

One syllable:	bus, plane, train, cat, truck
Two syllables:	paper, pencil, rubber, ruler
Three syllables:	spaghetti, tomato, pineapple, banana
Four syllables:	television, technology, Victoria, Australia
Five syllables:	hippopotamus, examination, inspirational

You will know how many syllables are in a word by clapping the beat.

book pa per pot a to hel i cop ter Scan din a vi a

Syllables can be **stressed** or **unstressed**.
Stressed syllables are pronounced with more emphasis than unstressed syllables. That is, we say that part of the word a little louder.

All one-syllable words are stressed.
In two-syllable words, either the first or the second syllable can be stressed: paper pencil because dessert.
In three-syllable words, either the first or the second syllable can be stressed: potato computer pineapple calendar yesterday).

TRY THIS

Underline the stressed syllable in these words.

chil dren	Sat ur day	bask et	re port er	ti ger
vol ca no	Chi na	con tain er	doc tor	hol i day
tad pole	trou ble some	ex plore	jag u ar	a bove

CLOSED SYLLABLES

When a syllable ends in a consonant, blend or buddy, the vowel is **closed in** and often has a short sound. For example:

pump kin	chick en	but ton
tick et	cus tard	rub bish
pos sum	pen cil	traf fic

OPEN SYLLABLES

When a syllable ends in a vowel, the vowel is **open** and has a long sound.

ti ger	ba con	ta ble
mo tel	ra dar	o ver
le ver	lo cal	pro gram

Say these two-syllable words.
Notice how the first vowel has a long sound.

flavour	paper	moment	grocer	basin
stolen	final	famous	private	secret
pretence	motor	solo	plural	stupid

HOW TO LEARN SPELLING

Spelling Sound-by-Sound

Here is a way to help you spell a word, letter-by-letter, by listening to the sounds.

1 Start by saying the word. **dog**

2 Listen to the sounds you can hear.

3 Say the word again, stretching out the sounds. **d – o – g**

4 Snap the word back together.

5 Write a letter for each sound you hear. **dog**

6 Check. Were you right?

7 If you are wrong, you will need to 'sound out' the word again.

Remember: A sound may be more than one letter, and don't forget the **silent e.**

d - u - s - t   r - ai - n   g - a - t - e

Strengthen your learning of a word this way by remembering what the word looks like.

Spelling Syllable-by-Syllable

Here is a way to help you learn to spell words, syllable by syllable.

1 Start by saying the word and listening to the beats in the word. — **volcano**

2 Count the beats (syllables) in the word.

3 Draw a box for each syllable.

4 Write each syllable in a box. — vol | ca | no

5 Say the word as you run your finger under the boxes.

6 Close your eyes and picture the letter sequence in each box.

7 Now write the word from your memory.

8 Check. Does it look right?

9 You may need to study the word again.

10 Remember, always write from your memory.

HOW TO LEARN SPELLING

Spelling from Memory

Here is a way to help you to remember how to spell words correctly.

1 Start by writing the word in large letters. **done**

2 Look at the word and say it 2 or 3 times.

3 Close your eyes and picture the word.

4 Open your eyes and check. Were you right?

5 Close your eyes and picture the word again.

6 Write it in the air with your finger.

7 Open your eyes and check. Were you right?

8 Now write the word on paper from memory.

9 Check. Were you right?

10 If you are wrong, you will need to study the word again.

11 Remember, always write from your memory.

Core Words with Constant Spelling

Many words in English remain constant in their spelling. We use these words over and over again in speaking and writing. These are the words that cement our ideas together.

These words include:

- prepositions – above, below, under, at, with…
- personal pronouns – I, you, he, him, she, her, it…
- possessive pronouns – my, his, hers, ours, their….
- relative pronouns – who, whom, whose, which, that
- articles – a, an, the
- demonstrative adjectives – this, that, these, those
- indefinite adjectives – some, many, few, any
- the verb 'helpers' – am, is, are, was were….
- some adverbs – there, here, before, after, not, very…
- conjunctions – when, or, so , but, because, whenever…

Note: Prefixes and suffixes are also constant in their spelling.

Added to this are a large number of words which are also used frequently in English. Unlike the words that are constant in their spelling, these words may vary according to the texts we are composing. For example: He looks well. I am looking at the clouds.

BASE WORDS

When you write stories, letters, or reports, you will notice that many words ALWAYS have the same spelling – words like the, put, over, where and by.

Many words ALWAYS have the same spelling.

You will also notice that you must change some words, so that what you write sounds right and makes sense.

You **would not** write:
The six boy are go for a walk in comfort shoe.
You **would** write:
The six boys are going for a walk in comfortable shoes.
You **would not** write:
The fun clown perform two danger stunt fear.
You **would** write:
The funny clown performed two dangerous stunts fearless*ly*.

These changes are most often made by adding an ending to the base word.

boy	+	s	go	+	ing	
comfort	+	able	funn	+	y	
perform	+	ed	stunt	+	s	
danger	+	ous	fear	+	less	+ ly

We can also change words by placing a syllable in front of the base word. For example: happy unhappy; appear disappear

TRY THIS

Change the base words by adding a beginning or an ending.

eat + ing	______________	un + tie	______________
box + es	______________	dis + like	______________
laugh + ed	______________	mis + behave	______________
care + less	______________	re + turn	______________
act + ive	______________	up + stairs	______________
music + ian	______________	down + stairs	______________

COMMON ENDINGS

one hat

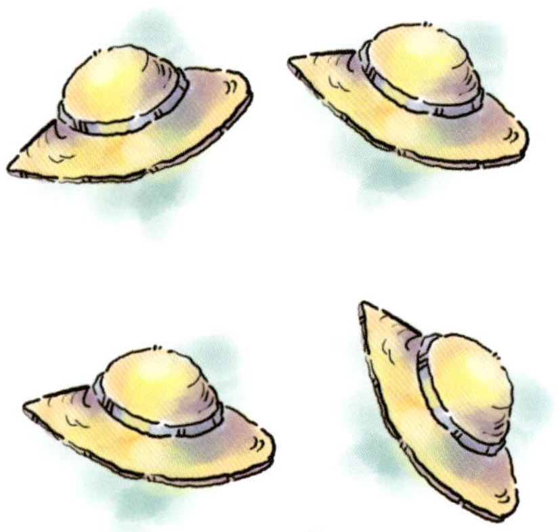
many hats

Writers add endings to certain types of words so that what they write sounds right and makes sense. Some of these endings are used so often, they are called **common endings**.
These endings are:
ing ed s es er est y ly

These endings are used to:

- Give number to common nouns (one apple, two apples; one peach, two peaches; one bus, several buses; one hat, many hats; one box, lots of boxes) *(See Plural Nouns, pages 50-57)*
- Give number to verbs (I jump, you jump, but he jumps and she jumps) *(See Present Tense Verbs, page 43)*
- Show the tense of verbs (I jump, I am jumping (*present tense*); I jumped (*past tense*). I play, I am playing, I played.) *(See Verb Tense, pages 43-44)*
- Change nouns to adjectives (rain, rainy; storm, stormy; grass, grassy; fun, funny; laze lazy) *(See Rules, pages 45,46)*
- Change adjectives to adverbs (neat, neatly; happy, happily; safe, safely) *(See Rules, pages 46,47)*
- Compare adjectives (tall, taller, tallest; long, longer, longest)
- Compare adverbs (high, higher, highest; fast, faster, fastest)

Add common endings to the underlined words.

Jackson is a soccer play____ . His Dad think____ he is the best play____ in the team. At the game on Saturday, Jackson kick____ three goal____ before half time. Ten minute____ into the second half, he was rush____ towards the goal post, dribbling the ball expert____ with his feet. Sudden____, a play____ from the other team push____ him aside rough____. He crash____ to the ground, hurt____ both his knee____. He stood up slow____ . He felt dizzy and sick as he limp____ off the field.

VERBS

It is usually the verbs that indicate when things are happening in text — present time, past time or future time. We call this verb tense.

Verbs indicate when things happen in text.

PRESENT TENSE VERBS

- **s** is added to a base verb to show present tense if the subject is a single person or thing and the text is being written from a third person point of view. For example: Jane likes jelly beans.
  A horse eats oats and hay.
  The sun rises every morning. He swims fast.
  A spider spins a web. She cooks pies.
- **es** is added to a base verb ending in the letter y to show present tense. In most cases, y is changed to i before adding es. For example: cry, cries; fly, flies; spy, spies; dry, dries; identify, identifies.
  Always add **es** to the words go and do (goes, does).
- **ing** is added to verbs to show present tense. The base verb always needs a 'helper' such as is, was, are or were. For example:
  Sarah is going to the movies.
  Bob was playing chess.
  The children are reading books.
  They were eating soup.

We most often add s or ing to the base verb to show present tense: He jumps. He is jumping.

TRY THIS

Add the correct ending to complete the verbs to show present tense.

Kara walk__ to school with Jess, but Jake ride__ his bike.

Jeff is read____ a book and I am do____ maths.

When the bell ring__, the teacher tell__ us to go out to lunch.

PAST TENSE VERBS

When we write about events that have already happened, we write in the past tense.
We add **ed** to the base verb to show past tense in a regular way. For example:
Sue walked home. Mum played golf.
He waited for the bus. Dad baked a cake.
Kylie watched TV. Tim ironed his shirt.

Write these verbs in the past tense. *(See Spelling Rules, pages 45-47)*

dust ______	plug ______	shop ______
pack ______	limp ______	buzz ______
race ______	cross ______	play ______
blink ______	hurry ______	slice ______
carry ______	trick ______	end ______

Many verbs show past tense in an irregular way. The base verb actually changes in its spelling.
eg run, ran; sleep, slept; do, did; blow, blew

Write the irregular past tense of these verbs.

Today	*Yesterday*	*Today*	*Yesterday*
grow	______	catch	______
ride	______	fly	______
fight	______	throw	______
eat	______	meet	______
steal	______	make	______
drink	______	buy	______
take	______	feed	______

1 Doubling

When a syllable contains a short vowel followed by one consonant, that consonant is doubled before adding an ending.

This is to protect the short vowel sound.

run, running; hop, hopping; skip, skipping

BUT jump, jumping

Say the word.
Find the vowel. Is it short? – Yes
How many letters follow the vowel - one or two?
Double the letter if there is one.
Do not double if there are two.

Remember: The doubling rule applies only to syllables with short vowels followed by one consonant.

Use the doubling rule when adding these common endings:

ing ed er est y

For example:			
	shop	shopping	shopped
	pack	packing	packed
	big	bigger	biggest
	long	longer	longest
	fun	funny	

Add endings to these words. Apply the doubling rule.

Base verb	Add **ing**	Add **ed**
trap		
hiss		
drag		
pat		
lick		

Base word	Add **er**	Add **est**
strong		
fat		
rich		
thin		
hot		

SPELLING RULES

2 Words Ending in e

Drop the e before adding an ending beginning with a vowel or the letter y.

ride	hope	shine	fame	safe	fine
riding	hoped	shiny	famous	safer	finest

Keep the e before adding an ending beginning with a consonant.

use	close	amaze	pale	safe	price
useful	closely	amazement	paleness	safety	priceless

TRY THIS

Apply the rules for words ending in e to add endings to these words.

bake + ing	________	like + ed	________	slime + y	________
lone + ly	________	tribe + al	________	state + ment	________
tune + ful	________	home + less	________	shake + ing	________
shade + y	________	smile + ed	________	tube + s	________
place + ing	________	wise + ly	________	vote + ed	________

Add an ending to the words in the boxes to complete the sentences correctly. Apply the rules for words ending in e.

When everyone left, he felt ______________. lone

We thought the story was very ______________. amuse

The crowd went wild as the ________ came on stage. sing

He ______________ the empty box to store his toys. use

The pizza was hot and ______________. spice

SPELLING RULES

3 Words Ending in y

If the letter before the y is a consonant, change the y to i and add es.
For example:

baby, babies   dry, dries   lady, ladies   cry, cries

If the letter before the y is a vowel, just add s. For example:

boy, boys   day, days   toy, toys   play, plays

Write the plural form of these words. Apply the rule for words ending in y.

body	________	monkey	________
chimney	________	bunny	________
fairy	________	tray	________
holiday	________	melody	________
story	________	donkey	________
country	________	key	________

Add s or es to form present tense verbs. Apply the rule for words ending in y.

pay	________	spy	________
cry	________	enjoy	________
buy	________	pray	________
try	________	fly	________
stay	________	employ	________

4 Words Ending in f

Follow these two simple rules to write the plural of nouns ending in f.

1. **If you hear the f in the noun plural, just add s.**
   eg roof roofs
2. **If you hear v in the noun plural, change the f to v and add es.**
   eg self selves

Write the plural form of these words.

shelf	________	hoof	________
roof	________	knife	________
chief	________	reef	________
calf	________	belief	________
giraffe	________	wolf	________
self	________	life	________

When changing a noun ending in f to a verb, you will need to change the f to v and add e:

thief, thieve relief, relieve

Applying the same rule, change these words to verbs.

strife	________	proof	________
grief	________	life	________
safe	________	belief	________

5 i Before e Except After c

In words where ie represents the long e sound, i is generally before the e.
For example: piece siege field

However, the e is written before the i after a c.
For example: receive ceiling conceited

TRY THIS

Put in the missing letters, ie or ei.
Apply the above rule.

gr _ _ f	ach _ _ ve	rec _ _ ve	retr _ _ ve	dec _ _ ve
bel _ _ ve	rec _ _ pt	hyg _ _ ne	conc _ _ t	n _ _ ce
f _ _ rce	bes _ _ ge	dec _ _ t	perc _ _ ve	p _ _ r
br _ _ f	c _ _ ling	rel _ _ f	th _ _ ve	ch _ _ f

Here are some exceptions to this general rule:

their geisha protein seize weir
weird caffeine species foreign forfeit

PLURAL NOUNS

Plural nouns add s or es to the singular noun.

Common nouns can name one thing (singular) or more than one thing (plural). We show plural nouns by adding s or es to the singular noun.

1 horse, 2 horses; 1 dish, many dishes; a dot, lots of dots

Most of the time we just add s to the singular noun to form the plural.
For example: houses bells trees elephants rivers biscuits lemons boats

We add es to nouns that end in ch, sh, x, s, ss or zz.
For example: foxes benches wishes buses kisses lunches lashes quizzes

TRY THIS

Add s or es to form the plural of these nouns.

candle__	dish__	dancer__	apple__
beach__	comb__	match__	leash__
dress__	stone__	cross__	tax__
gas__	cup__	robot__	trumpet__

We usually add s to nouns ending in o, but there are some to which we add es.

Add s		Add es	
piano	pianos	tornado	tornadoes
solo	solos	volcano	volcanoes
photo	photos	tomato	tomatoes
kangaroo	kangaroos	potato	potatoes
radio	radios	echo	echoes
silo	silos	hero	heroes
cockatoo	cockatoos	cargo	cargoes
cello	cellos	embargo	embargoes
cappuccino	cappuccinos	avocado	avocadoes

REGULAR AND IRREGULAR PLURALS

The plural form of most common nouns is formed by adding **s** or **es** to the singular noun. These are regular plurals.

Some plural nouns, however, are irregular and require a change of spelling.

tooth, teeth goose, geese

Write the plural form of these words. All are irregular.

child ________ man ________

mouse ________ tooth ________

woman ________ foot ________

Irregular plurals are usually listed in a dictionary after the singular noun.

Some words we use come from foreign languages. We use both their singular and plural forms. Here are some examples:

bacterium, bacteria	axis, axes	platypus, platypuses	campus, campuses
medium, media, mediums	crisis, crises	octopus, octopuses	terminus, termini
datum, data	oasis, oases	virus, viruses	stimulus, stimuli
alga, algae	radius, radii	criterion, criteria	ellipsis, ellipses
larva, larvae	fungus, fungi	phenomenon, phenomena	basis, bases

- Add **s** to form the plurals of most abbreviated words and acronyms (DVDs, CDs, VIPs, Drs (doctors), 1920s, DJs, tspns)
- Doubling a letter makes some abbreviations plural (p (page), pp (pages))
- Some words are both singular and plural (fish, sheep, deer)
- Some words are only plural (jeans, trousers, scissors, rice, spaghetti, rain, snow, sunlight, moonlight, garbage, cutlery)

PLURAL VERBS

Many verbs have singular and plural forms.

She likes apples. They like oranges.

In the simple present tense, many singular verbs end in **s**, but plural verbs do not.

She eats pasta. They eat pizza.
He keeps birds. They keep bees.

TRY THIS

Complete the sentences. Add an s where necessary.

like	She _____ peas.	They _____ pies.
swim	He _____ in a pool.	They _____ in the dam.
plant	He _____ a tree.	We _____ trees.
ride	She _____ home.	They _____ home.

Some verbs have different singular and plural forms.

Singular: I am. She is. He is. It is.
Plural: We are. They are.

Singular: I was. She was. He was. It was.
Plural: We were. They were.

Singular: He has. She has. It has.
Plural: We have. They have.

Singular verbs need a singular subject and plural verbs need a plural subject.

Jackson (subject) has fifty dollars.
His brothers (subject) have twenty.

The wild pig (subject) was terrified.
The hunters (subject) were right behind it.

Subject and verb must ALWAYS agree.

PRONOUNS

The spelling of pronouns is always the same BUT there is a singular and a plural form, and a possessive form to show ownership.

SINGULAR	POSSESSIVE	PLURAL	POSSESSIVE
I, me	my, mine	we, us	our, ours
you	yours	you	yours
he, him	his	they, them	their, theirs
she, her	her, hers	they, them	their, theirs

The pronouns **I**, **he**, **she**, **we** and **they** are used in **subject** position.

I like pizza.
Jack and I like pineapple.
He likes pasta.
She likes pepperoni.
We like peanuts and popcorn.
They like peas, potatoes and pumpkin.

The pronouns **me**, **him**, **her**, **us** and **them** are used in **object** position.

Jo gave me a banana.
Jo gave him an apple.
Jo gave her a peach.
Jo gave us a watermelon.
Jo gave them a bag of oranges.

Possessive pronouns – my, mine, his, her, hers, our, ours, their, theirs.

This is my book. It is mine.
This is his computer game. It is his.
This is her watch. It is hers.
These are our model planes. They are ours.
These are their marbles. They are theirs.

PERSON

Person is a term used to describe three different forms of pronouns. They are:
first, second and third person.

First Person
The speaker, writer or character is relating the events and uses first-person pronouns.
I me my mine we us our ours

Second Person
The speaker, writer or character is talking to another person or persons and uses second-person pronouns.
you your yours

Third Person
The speaker or writer or character is talking about other people and things and uses third-person pronouns.
he him his she her hers it its they them their theirs

Decide whether these sentences are written in the first, second or third person.

Will you take your dog for a walk? ____________

They left yesterday to visit their uncle. ____________

We wanted them to come with us. ____________

You must learn your spelling. ____________

I waited, but my bus did not arrive. ____________

CAPITAL LETTERS

Words begin with capital letters for a number of reasons:

- First word in a sentence:
  The game is over. Open the window. There is my friend. Wait for my sister.
- First word in direct speech:
  The teacher said, "Pass your books to me please."
  Dan said, "Mine is at home."
- Names of people and pets:
  Sally, Fred, Anjana, Pepper, Rusty
- Names of titled people:
  Princess Mary, Dr Philips, Sir Henry Alford, Lord Byron
- Names of places of work, business and entertainment:
  Myer, K-Mart, Dreamworld, Scots College, Empire Theatre
- Names of days of the week and months of the year:
  Thursday, Friday, April, August
- Names of countries, states and cities:
  India, England, Victoria, Iowa, Brisbane, Paris, London
- Names of geographical features:
  Swan River, Mount Everest, Lake Ontario, Sahara Desert, Niagara Falls
- Names of man-made structures:
  Sydney Harbour Bridge, Eiffel Tower, Statue of Liberty
- Names of special events:
  Easter, Ramadan, Anzac Day, River Festival, Red Nose Day
- Names of newspapers, books, magazines, films and songs:
  Lord of the Rings, The Lion, the Witch and the Wardrobe, Advance Australia Fair, The Age, Women's Weekly (NOTE: Only the important words are given a capital letter.)
- Brand names:
  Toyota, Cadbury, Microsoft, Nike
- Names of nationalities and religions:
  Chinese, Swiss, Polish, Judaism, Islam, Christianity

Whole words can be written in capital letters for emphasis. eg I am SO excited! You did WHAT?

THE APOSTROPHE

An apostrophe is used with nouns to show ownership.
Jeremy's scooter   My friend's photo

DO NOT use an apostrophe with a pronoun to show ownership. Pronouns have their own possessive form.

- Place the apostrophe after the **singular noun** and add **s**.
  dog - dog's bone; cat - cat's whiskers; builder - builder's tools;
  Mary's lunch; Grandpa's beard; Tom's coat; my sister's pets
- Place the apostrophe after a **regular plural noun**.
  pigs – pigs' food; ladies – ladies' dresses; chickens – chickens' feathers;
  teachers' staffroom; owls' eyes; horses' hoofs; cars' motors; birds' nests
- Place the apostrophe after an **irregular plural noun** and add **s**.
  children – children's games; men – men's clothes; women – women's scarves

TRY THIS

Make the underlined nouns possessive, using the information above.

We could see the tractor in the farmer____ field.
These are James____ library books.
I could hear the drumming of kangaroos____ feet.
Rain trickled off the riders____ helmets.
We waited and waited for John____ dad to come.
The teacher smiled at the girls____ funny animal masks.
There was a large ant____ nest under the tree.
Sun shone on the dragonflies____ wings.
His foot got caught in his bike____ wheel.

If a singular noun ends in s, you can just add an apostrophe.

CONTRACTIONS

An apostrophe is used to mark shortened phrases called **contractions**.
It shows where letters have been left out.
you are = you're   is not = isn't

Contractions are used in speech and in informal writing.

Here is a list of some everyday contractions.

I am	*I'm*	we have	*we've*	what is	*what's*
I have	*I've*	we had	*we'd*	what has	*what's*
I had	*I'd*	we would	*we'd*	who is	*who's*
I would	*I'd*	we will	*we'll*	who has	*who's*
I will	*I'll*	let us	*let's*	who have	*who've*
you are	*you're*	could have	*could've*	who would	*who'd*
you have	*you've*	should have	*should've*	who will	*who'll*
you had	*you'd*	would have	*would've*	shall not	*shan't*
you would	*you'd*	here is	*here's*	will not	*won't*
you will	*you'll*	there is	*there's*	can not	*can't*
it is; it has	*it's*	there has	*there's*	could not	*couldn't*
it would	*it'd*	there had	*there'd*	do not	*don't*
it had	*it'd*	there would	*there'd*	does not	*doesn't*
it will	*it'll*	there will	*there'll*	did not	*didn't*
that is	*that's*	he is	*he's*	is not	*isn't*
that has	*that's*	he has	*he's*	has not	*hasn't*
that will	*that'll*	he had	*he'd*	have not	*haven't*
that had	*that'd*	he would	*he'd*	had not	*hadn't*
that would	*that'd*	she will	*he'll*	was not	*wasn't*
she is	*she's*	they are	*they're*	were not	*weren't*
she has	*she's*	they have	*they've*	has not	*hasn't*
she had	*she'd*	they had	*they'd*	have not	*haven't*
she would	*she'd*	they would	*they'd*	are not	*aren't*
she will	*she'll*	they will	*they'll*		
we are	*we're*	where is	*where's*		

Complete the sentences using a contraction for the phrase.

He _____________ come in out of the rain. (would not)
They ___________ seen the movie yet. (have not)
__________ like to go for a picnic in the bush. (we would)
She _____________ run as fast as me. (could not)

COMPOUND WORDS

Two words joined together make a compound word.

corn + flakes = cornflakes
tea + pot = teapot
sun + shine = sunshine
tea + spoon = teaspoon

Read these words. Find the two words that make the compound word and put a line between them.

bath|room	bedroom	waterfall
padlock	lunchbox	bullfrog
cowshed	seesaw	flashlight
haystack	whenever	raindrops
schoolbag	crosspatch	mudpie
pinstripe	whiteboard	bluebird
notebook	notepaper	wishbone
snakeskin	gemstone	penknife
pushbike	framework	show-off
timetable	bridegroom	carwash
railway	wheelbarrow	wheelchair
plaything	paintbrush	stopwatch
sleepover	aftershock	spotlight
farmyard	daydream	postcard
roadway	mailbox	throwaway
takeaway	mousetrap	horseshoe
newspaper	downstairs	soundwaves
eyebrow	downstream	nursemaid
cowbell	cowboy	girlfriend
boyfriend	mouthorgan	walkway
screwdriver	timepiece	thunderstorm
shoreline	knockout	torchlight
headgear	headwear	bare-headed

HOMONYMS

Homonyms have the same sound or spelling

Homonyms are words with the same sound or spelling, but different meanings.

There are two types of homonyms – homographs and homophones.

homo- (same) + graph (writing)
homo- (same) + phone (sound)

Homographs are words that have the same spelling, but different meanings.

Let me shake your hand.
Hand me a fork please.

She threw a rock in the pond.
He will rock the baby to sleep.

I know the answer is right.
Turn right at the next corner.

We took the lift to the top floor.
He could not lift the heavy bricks.

Think about at least two meanings for each of these words.

train strike block well back watch rose table rest palm
duck blind state spring match

TRY THIS

Write one word that would make each pair of sentences make sense.

He struck a ________ to light the candle.
Who won the tennis ________?

She had to _______ under the low branch.
A _______ waddled down to the pond.

Did you _______ the game on TV?
It is six o'clock by my _________.

He twisted his ________ ankle.
The plane _______ Perth at two o'clock.

HOMOGRAPHS

Did he refuse to play with you?

Place all refuse in the bin.

Homographs include words with the same spelling, but are pronounced differently and have different meanings.

Did you tear your shirt?
I saw a tear in his eye.

I need to wind my old wall clock.
The wind blew the leaves off the trees.

He lives close by.
Did you close the window?

I wound my old wall clock.
He put a bandage over the wound.

He set a new speed bike record.
The singer will record her new song.

TRY THIS

Think of one word that would make each pair of sentences make sense. Note how each word is pronounced differently.

I opened my birthday _________.
He will _______ the girl with a certificate.

She tied her hair ribbon into a ________.
He had to _____ before his queen.

I will ______ my boat across the dam.
Jenny had a ______ with her big sister.

They _____ the news about the robbery in the paper.
Did you ______ about the robbery in the paper?

I live in a brick _______ in the suburbs.
They will ______ the students in several dormitories.

HOMOPHONES

Homophones are words that have the same sound but are spelt differently and have different meanings.

She rode her bike down the road to school.

Here are four oranges for you to eat.

He ate more than eight jelly beans.

Think about how you would use these homophones.

by, buy	blue, blew	meet, meat	paw, poor
sun, son	hair, hare	flour, flower	one, won
steal, steel	sure, shore	be, bee	new, knew

Underline the correct word to complete each sentence.

TRY THIS

I will (great, grate) cheese to top the pizza.

Kerri bought a pair of jeans at (sail, sale) price.

I stood on a stone and my (heel, heal) is (saw, sore).

We walked across the sand in (bear, bare) feet.

The workers are busy at the building (site, sight).

He wanted a (pair, pear) and an apple for lunch.

The lion prowls in search of (pray, prey).

This is a (tail, tale) about an enchanted forest.

If you are not sure which homophone to select, check the dictionary. Most dictionaries identify homophones.

ANTONYMS

Antonyms are words opposite in meaning to each other.

hot cold   long short   high low   up down

Writers use antonyms to show contrasts between characters, settings and events.

Can you match up these everyday antonyms?

old	tame	fat	wet	early	soft	in	right
slow	short	dry	go	night	stale	above	female
tall	sick	right	thin	hard	little	loud	below
well	young	smooth	wrong	big	day	left	soft
wild	fast	come	rough	fresh	late	male	out

Many antonyms are formed by adding the prefixes:
un dis mis im ir il
happy, unhappy; like ,dislike; print, misprint; proper, improper; legal, illegal; regular, irregular

Complete the antonyms by adding a prefix. Choose from un, dis and mis.

____ appear	____ locate	____ clean
____ tie	____ judge	____ allow
____ place	____ true	____ use
____ usual	____ understand	____ agree
____ read	____ obey	____ lead

PREFIXES

A prefix is a syllable attached to the beginning of a word. It changes the meaning of the word.

like, dislike; lock, unlock; turn, return

Prefixes are ALWAYS spelt in the same way.

A number of prefixes change a word to an antonym.

anti-	**de-**	**dis-**	**il-**	**in-**
anticlockwise	deport	disappear	illegal	incapable
antisocial	destabilise	disobey	illogical	invisible
antiperspirant	debrief	discourage	illiterate	informal
im-	**ir-**	**mis-**	**non-**	**un-**
impossible	irregular	misjudge	nonviolent	unclean
impatient	irrelevant	mispronounce	non-smoking	untrue
imperfect	irreplaceable	misfortune	nonplus	unuseful

Add the prefixes given and say the new words.

pre *(before)*	after *(afterwards)*	fore *(in front)*	semi *(half)*
cooked	noon	runner	circle
judge	shave	front	final
historic	thought	warn	conscious
caution	taste	cast	precious
arrange	shock	ground	colon

SUFFIXES

TRY THIS

A suffix is a syllable attached to the end of a word. It changes the way the word is used.

attract attraction attractive attractively

The suffixes **ful** and **less** create words of opposite meaning.

Complete the antonyms.

helpful	helpless	doubt	doubt
use	use	power	power
care	care	thought	thought
rest	rest	colour	colour

Add the suffixes given.
Apply rules for words ending in e and y.

impress + ion	____________	busy + ness	____________
serve + ice	____________	educate + ion	____________
fool + ish	____________	familiar + ise	____________
rely + able	____________	tire + some	____________
appoint + ment	____________	race + ist	____________
secure + ity	____________	social + ise	____________
nerve + ous	____________	amuse + ment	____________
partner + ship	____________	perform + ance	____________

- Some words require bigger changes in spelling and pronunciation (private, privacy; conclude, conclusion; terror, terrify; compete, competition).
- You can add more than one suffix to a word (manage, manager, managerial; use, useless, uselessness; form, formal, formally).
- You can add a prefix and a suffix to a word (accurate, inaccuracy; place, displacement; question, unquestionable).

LATIN & GREEK ROOTS

Many families of words have grown from Latin and Greek roots, like a family tree.

(Latin) **porto** = I carry
porter portable export import
transport report

(Greek) **tele** = at a distance
telephone television telegraph
telescope

Here are some other Latin and Greek roots:

LATIN

- annus = a year: annual, annuity, bienniel, annals, anniversary, centennial, trienniel
- facio = I make, do: fact, factual, faction, factory, facile, facility, fashion
- aequus = equal: equal, equate, equable, equality, equitable, equivalent, equity, inequity, adequate, equilateral, equator
- verto = I turn: vertical, convert, converse, convertible, revert, reverse, invert, inverse, introvert, extrovert
- sentio = I feel: sense, sensation, sensible, senseless, nonsense, sentence, sentiment, assent, dissent, consent

GREEK

- grapho = I write: graph, graphic, graphite, autograph, telegraph, paragraph, cinematograph, biography, autobiography, geography, bibliography, photography
- pathos = feeling: pathos, pathetic, sympathy, empathy, antipathy, apathy
- monos = alone: monopoly, monopolise, monogram, monoplane, monotype, monocle
- thermos = heat: thermal, thermometer, thermostat, thermos
- scopeo = I see: scope, telescope, microscope, periscope

ABBREVIATIONS

Abbreviations are shortened forms of words. Writers save time (and space) by using them.
St - Street; Mr - Mister; eg - for example; Sat - Saturday

There are different types of abbreviations:

- Abbreviations that consist of the first one or more letters of the full word (p – page; Vic – Victoria; Co – Company; Ave – Avenue).
- Abbreviations that start with the first letter and end with the last letter of the full word (ck – creek; bros – brothers; hwy – highway).
- Abbreviations of Latin words (am – ante meridiem (before noon); (et al – et alii (and others); no – numero (number)).
- Contractions (can't – cannot; o'er – over; wouldn't – would not).
- Abbreviations made up of shortened forms of other words (bus – omnibus; chips – chipped potatoes; budgie – budgerigar; email – electronic mail).
- Abbreviations of letters and numbers used in text messaging (SMS- Short Message Service) (ASAP - as soon as possible; L8R – later; B4N – bye for now; UR – you are; F2F – face to face; LOL – laugh out loud).

An **acronym** is a type of abbreviation. Acronyms are constructed by joining the first letters of a group of words. They are spoken either as a word, or by their letter names.
ANZAC – Australian and New Zealand Army Corps;
radar – radio detecting and ranging;
QANTAS – Queensland and Northern Territory Air Service; TV – television

TRY THIS

What words have been shortened in these abbreviations?

QLD	mL	Dr	fax	kg
croc	DVD	min	Apr	c
Uni	km	limo	ff (in music)	VIP
GB (in computing)	hr	SA	kj	CU (SMS)

PROOFREADING

Whenever we write text, we need to go back and check that our spelling is correct.

When you proofread, you are simply trying to spot any errors in spelling **with your eyes**.

Run your finger under each line of writing and look at each word.
If one does not look right, check the spelling in a dictionary.

It is polite to give your reader writing that is free of spelling errors.

Can you spot and fix the eight spelling errors in this text?

Sunset came. The wind died down to a soft murmur in the gum trees outside. The fountin bubbled and splasht in the fishpond.
The wite ducks would be asleep, heads under wings. Peter Sox lit the fire. Bobbie Sox curled up with her knitting. Lulu sighed and wached her reflecshun in the windowpane. She looked quiet sunny in the firelight!
"Yellow cold be nice," she thought drowsyly and drifted off to sleep.

GUIDE TO SOUNDS IN ENGLISH

Here is a quick guide to the many sounds of spoken English and the different letters that represent them.

THE CONSONANTS

Sound	Spellings
b	**b** bed **bb** rabbit
c (k)	**c** cow **cc** occur **ch** chorus **k** kid **ck** sick **qu** bouquet
ch	**ch** chocolate **c** cello
d	**d** dog **dd** middle
f	**f** fat **ff** coffee **ph** phone **gh** rough
g	**g** girl **gg** egg **gh** ghost **gu** guest
h	**h** house **wh** who
j	**j** jeans **g** gym **dge** edge
l	**l** leg **ll** bell **le** table
m	**m** moon **mm** hammer **mb** comb
n	**n** not **nn** inn **kn** knee **gn** gnome
ng	**ng** sing **n** pink
p	**p** pan **pp** copper
r	**r** rat **rr** mirror **wr** write **rh** rhyme
s	**s** sit **ss** kiss **c** city **sc** scissors
sh (voiceless)	**sh** shop **sch** schedule **s** sugar **ss** tissue **sc** luscious **ch** machine **ce** ocean **ti** motion
sh (voiced)	**si** vision **s** measure **z** azure
t	**t** tap **tt** little **bt** doubt **pt** receipt **th** thyme
th (voiceless)	**th** thing
th (voiced)	**th** this
v	**v** very **f** of
w	**w** went **wh** wharf
y	**y** yet
z	**z** zebra **zz** dizzy **s** rose **ss** scissors

SHORT VOWEL SOUNDS

Sound	Spellings
a	**a** cat **ai** plait
e	**e** pet **a** any **ea** bread **ei** heifer **ai** said
i	**i** zip **u** busy **y** gym **ie** sieve **o** women **ui** build **a** cottage
o	**o** pot **a** watch **ou** cough **au** auction
u	**u** cut **o** come **oo** flood **ou** trouble **ough** tough **a** away **au** aurora

Vowels are often marked in pronunciation guides:

Short vowels â ê î ô û

Long vowels ā ē ī ō ū

Schwa is an unstressed or neutral vowel sound heard in many words in English.
eg
a about **e** taken
i pencil **o** lemon
u circus **er** mother

It is often represented by **uh** in pronunciation guides.
eg temperature:
tem-pr**uh**-ch**uh**

LONG VOWELS AND VOWEL TEAMS

Sound	Spellings
a	**a** baby **a-e** game **ai** sail **ay** play **ey** they **ea** break **ei** rein **eigh** eight **é** cliché **et** ballet
ar	**ar** car **a** bath **au** laugh
air	**air** fair **are** care **eir** heir **ae** aeroplane **ear** bear
e	**e** event **e-e** theme **ee** feet **ea** seat **ie** chief **ei** ceiling **eo** people **ey** key **i** ski
er	**er** her **ear** learn **ir** bird **ur** curl **or** word **our** journal
i	**i** kind **i-e** ride **igh** high **ig** sign **y** fly **ey** eye **ie** pie **eigh** height **ai** aisle

Sound	Spellings
o	**o** both **o-e** bone **oe** toe **oa** boat **ow** low **oo** brooch **ou** soul **ough** dough **ew** sew **eau** beau
oi	**oi** boil **oy** boy
oo	**oo** cook **u** put **oul** could
or	**or** fork **ore** more **au** autumn **aw** straw **our** court **augh** taught **ough** bought **oar** board **oor** door **a** small **ar** warm
ou	**ou** loud **ow** cow **ough** drought
u (yoo)	**u-e** use **ew** new **u** emu **ue** avenue **eau** beauty
u (oo)	**u** ruby **u-e** flute **ue** blue **ui** juice **o** move **oo** cool **ou** group **ough** through **ew** flew

WORD ALERT! WORDS OFTEN CONFUSED

In English, many words are easily confused because of small differences in spelling. Always check a dictionary if you are not sure which word to use. Here are some particularly tricky ones.

accede **exceed**	to agree or consent (I accede to your wishes.) to go beyond something (Don't exceed the speed limit.)
accept **except** **expect**	take or receive something willingly (I accept your invitation.) leaving out, excluding (Everyone except me.) to look forward to (I expect him soon.)
affect **effect**	(usually a verb) to cause a change in something (His words affected us all.) (usually a noun) the result of something (His words had a great effect on us all.)
assure **ensure** **insure**	tell someone something with certainty (I assure you I will not be late.) make certain of something (Please ensure all doors are locked.) to arrange for the replacement of goods lost, damaged or stolen (I insured my car.)
bought **brought**	past tense of buy (I bought a new computer game yesterday.) past tense of bring (He brought his new computer game to show me.)
canvas **canvass**	heavy, woven cloth (The old tent was made from canvas.) to ask for votes or support from someone (He canvassed voters for their support)
cite **site**	to mention or refer to something as an example (He cited two cases of theft.) land where something is built or will be built (a building site)
continual **continuous**	happening often, but not all the time (The baby cried continually.) going on without stopping, like breathing (The water flowed continuously.)
coarse **course**	1. thick or rough (coarse sand) 2. crude or uncouth (a coarse person) 1. area where a race takes place (race course) 2. program (a course of study) 3. part of a meal (main course)
council **counsel**	government of a small area (City Council) 1. advice (noun) (to keep one's own counsel); 2. to advise (verb)(She counselled the students.)
currant **current**	small, dried, seedless grape 1. flow or movement of air, water, electricity (The electrical current was strong.) 2. up-to-date, now (At the current time.)
dairy **diary**	place where cows are milked (dairy products) book for recording daily events (He wrote in his diary every day.)
desert **dessert**	1. dry, sandy place (Simpson Desert) 2. run away from; abandon (The soldier deserted the battle.) sweet dish served at the end of a meal (I love dessert.)
deceased **diseased**	no longer living (My grandfather is deceased.) infected with a disease (The trees were diseased.)
die **dye**	1. stop living (He died) 2. metal tool for cutting objects (he used a die) to colour, colouring (She dyed the cloth with blue dye.)
disinterested **uninterested**	not personally involved; having no bias or self-interest in something (a disinterested party) opposite of interested (I was uninterested in the topic)
draft **draught**	rough sketch or piece of writing (a first draft) (pronounced draft) current of air (a draughty room)
enquiry **inquiry**	You can use either spelling, but enquiry usually relates to a question and inquiry to an investigation. (She enquired about how the inquiry went.)

eminent **imminent**	important or high in rank (eminent surgeon) likely to happen at any moment (Lightning warned us a storm was imminent.)
fewer **less**	refers to things you can count (fewer people; fewer chairs) refers to things you can't count (less water; less sugar)
formally **formerly**	following official or proper procedure (I formally thanked her for her gift.) previously; in the past (The actor was formerly a taxi driver.)
good **well**	refers to nouns (good luck; good friends; good idea) refers to verbs (they work well; she sings well; he ran well) You look well (health). You look good (looks).
later **latter**	some time in the future (See you later. Let's eat later. Come back later.) the second of two (Of apples and oranges, I prefer the latter. [oranges])
larva **lava**	a young insect before it changes form (A caterpillar is the larva of a butterfly.) hot melted rock which comes from a volcano (Lava flowed down the mountain.)
leant **lent**	past tense of lean (He leant on his walking stick.) past tense of lend (He lent me five dollars.)
lightening **lightning**	to make less dark or less in weight (He is lightening the colour of the paint.) electrical flash in the sky during a thunderstorm (The lightning was spectacular.)
mare **mayor**	a female horse (The mare has a foal.) leader of a local government (the city's mayor)
passed **past**	past tense of pass (She passed me her photos. Dad passed the slow car.) past years (adjective) in the past (noun) a dog ran past (adverb) past the window (preposition)
practice **practise**	(noun) action or performance (She does her piano practice every day.) (verb) to do something in order to improve (He will practise his golf swing.)
precede **proceed**	to go before (pre = before) (He preceded her into the room.) to go forward (The meeting will proceed after lunch.)
quiet **quite**	opposite of noisy; calm, silent, restful (Be quiet!; a quiet weekend; a quiet child) considerably; somewhat (quite sick; quite old; quite long)
rung **wrung**	1.a step on a ladder 2. past participle of ring (The phone has rung three times.) twist or squeeze something (She wrung the water out of the clothes.)
remember **reminisce**	to recall something in your mind (I remember his name but not his face.) to recall past times (She likes to reminisce about her childhood days.)
story **storey**	a relating of events, real or imaginary (fairy story) one whole level or floor of a building (Narrow stairs led us to the second storey.)
suit **suite**	1. a set of clothes (She wore a suit.) 2. one of four sets in a pack of cards (the suit of Clubs) 3. to be convenient (It will suit me to come tomorrow.) 4. a legal action (She brought a law suit against him.) a set of things, of furniture or rooms (a bedroom suite; the bridal suite)
vain **vane** **vein**	very proud of yourself, especially about the way you look (You're so vain.) a blade on a windmill (A weathervane shows the direction of the wind.) one of the small tubes that carries blood through the body (You could see the veins in his arm.)
wander **wonder**	to roam about going nowhere in particular (She wandered around the mall.) to think about something with curiosity or surprise (I wonder who'll come first.)
yoke **yolk**	1. collar worn by a horse for pulling carts (Like a yoke around my neck.) 2. part of a dress (The curved yoke flattered her neck.) yellow part of an egg (I like a runny yolk.)

FREQUENTLY MISSPELT WORDS

Here are 100 words that have been challenging spellers for years!

ache	done	making	they
again	don't	many	though
always	early	meant	through
among	easy	minute	tired
answer	enough	much	tonight
any	every	none	too
been	February	often	trouble
beginning	forty	once	Tuesday
believe	friend	piece	two
blue	guess	raise	used
break	half	ready	very
built	having	road	wear
business	hear	said	Wednesday
busy	heard	says	want
buy	here	seems	where
can't	hoarse	separate	whether
choose	hour	shoes	which
colour	instead	since	who
coming	just	some	whole
cough	knew	straight	women
could	know	sugar	won't
country	laid	sure	would
dear	library	tear	write
doctor	loose	their	writing
does	lose	there	wrote

SPELLING CHALLENGE

A quick look at those hard-to-spell words!

aboard
absurd
accelerate
accessory
accident
accommodation
acquaintance
aerial
amateur
ambition
anxiety
apologise
appreciate
article
assess
attendance
audience
auction
awkward
banquet
barbecue
bargain
bazaar
beautiful
beginning
behaviour
believe
beneficial
beverage
beyond
biscuit
blood
brief
brilliant
budget
bulletin
bureau
business
cabbage
campaign

cancelled
casual
caustic
ceiling
certain
chronological
circuit
column
committed
confidential
conscience
conscientious
conscious
convenient
courteous
counterfeit
criticism
damage
dangerous
decade
deceive
deficit
demolition
dependent
description
despair
detrimental
devastate
diamond
difference
disastrous
discipline
discussion
dissatisfied
draught
duct
eager
eccentric
edible
efficient

eighth
eligible
embarrass
eminent
emphatically
encore
encourage
exaggerate
exceed
excellent
exercise
exhausted
exhibition
experience
extension
extraordinary
fabulous
facial
facilities
familiar
fantastic
feasible
fifth
figure
financially
flourish
fluency
foreign
foremost
forfeit
friendliness
fulfill
fungus
future
gauge
gaunt
gauze
generally
generosity
genuine

geography
glacial
glossary
gondolier
government
gracious
grandeur
grievance
grocery
grotesque
guard
guerrilla
guidance
guilty
gymnasium
haphazard
harass
hastily
headache
healthy
heinous
heredity
hierarchy
hindrance
hippopotamus
honorable
horizon
horror
hosiery
hospitality
humour
hurriedly
hygiene
hypocrite
idea
ignition
imagine
immaculate
immediately
immigrant
imminent

implement
inability
incidentally
independent
inevitable
inhibit
insecurity
intelligent
interfere
interrupt
irrelevant
jaguar
jaunt
jockey
jostle
jovial
jubilant
judgment
judiciary
justice
kangaroo
kennel
kerosene
kindred
kiosk
knead
knight
knowledge
knuckle
koala
laboratory
lacquer
laughter
league
legacy
legible
legitimate
leisure
liability
license

SPELLING CHALLENGE Continued

licorice
liquefy
literature
location
locust
lounge
lubricate
luggage
luxury
lyric
macaroni
machine
magnificent
maintenance
majority
malice
mammoth
manacle
manageable
massage
mechanism
melancholy
melodious
menagerie
merchandise
metaphor
miniature
miscellaneous
mortgage
mosquito
multiple
myriad
nation
nature
nausea
nautical
nebular
necessary
negligible
negotiate

neither
neurotic
nicety
noticeable
notoriety
nourishment
novelist
noxious
nurture
nutrition
obedient
obscure
observatory
obsession
obsolete
obstacle
occasionally
occupant
occurrence
ominous
omission
opaque
opera
opinion
opportunity
orchestra
organism
orphan
oscillate
oxygen
palatial
palette
pamphlet
parallel
partially
particularly
patient
pauper
peninsula
period

persevere
personality
personnel
persuade
petroleum
physically
placard
pleasant
poise
possession
practical
precede
precious
preference
procedure
principal
principle
privacy
privilege
pronunciation
prophecy
punctual
quadrant
quality
quantity
quarantine
questionnaire
raisin
rarity
recede
receipt
recognise
recommend
recreation
recruit
religion
repellent
repetition
requirement
research

reservoir
resource
restaurant
rhythm
ridiculous
rivalry
scenery
schedule
science
scissors
secretary
signature
silence
simplicity
skillful
society
solemn
solution
spiral
stationary
suave
subtle
success
sufficient
surprise
susceptible
technique
temperature
tendency
tentacle
territory
thaw
theme
theory
thistle
thorough
tissue
tongue
touch
tradition

tranquil
transferred
treacherous
treasure
turquoise
typical
ulcer
unanimous
undoubtedly
uniform
university
unnecessary
unwieldy
upholsterer
urgency
usually
utensil
vacancy
vacuum
vague
valuable
various
vegetable
vehicle
versatile
villain
virus
wadding
wager
wanderer
warrant
weather
wholly
wreath
wrestler
yacht
yawn
yield
youthfulness
zodiac

HIGH-FREQUENCY WORDS

a
aboard
about
above
across
after
afterwards
again
against
ago
all
almost
along
alright
also
although
always
am
among
amongst
an
and
another
any
are
aren’t
around
as
at
away
because
been
before
behind
below
beneath
beside
between
both
but
by
came
can
can’t

could
couldn’t
could’ve
despite
did
didn’t
does
doesn’t
done
don’t
down
during
each
either
ever
every
everybody
everyone
everything
everywhere
for
forever
forthwith
from
gave
goes
gone
good
got
had
hadn’t
has
hasn’t
haven’t
he
he’d
he’s
he’ll
hence
henceforth
here
here’s
her
herself

him
himself
his
how
I
I’d
I’ll
I’m
I’ve
if
in
into
is
isn’t
it
its
it’d
it’s
it’ll
let’s
made
many
may
maybe
me
meanwhile
might
mine
more
moreover
much
must
my
myself
neither
never
nevertheless
next
no
not
nothing
nowhere
of

off
often
once
one
only
or
other
otherwise
ought
our
ours
ourselves
out
over
past
quite
said
saw
shall
shan’t
she
she’d
she’ll
she’s
should
should’ve
since
so
some
somebody
somehow
someone
something
sometimes
somewhat
somewhere
still
than
that
that’d
that’ll
that’s
the
their

theirs them
themselves
then
thence
there
there’d
there’ll
there’s
therefore
these
they
they’d
they’ll
they’re
they’ve
this
those
though
through
thus
till
to
too
took
towards
under
unless
until
up
upon
upwards
us
very
was
wasn’t
we
we’d
we’ll
we’re
we’ve
well
went
were

weren’t
what
what’s
whatever
when
whence
whenever
where
where’d
where’ll
where’s
wherever
whether
which
while
whilst
who
who’d
who’ll
who’s
whom
whose
why
why’s
will
with
without
won’t
would
would’ve
yes
yet
you
you’d
you’ll
your
you’re
yours
you’ve

MORE HIGH-FREQUENCY WORDS

able	drink	green	milk	ready	threw
air	early	hair	money	really	time
animal	earth	happy	month	red	today
aunt	east	have	moon	ride	told
ask	eat	hear	morning	right	tomorrow
baby	eight	heard	most	ring	town
back	empty	heavy	mother	road	train
ball	end	help	mouse	room	tree
be	enough	high	mum	round	turn
beautiful	even	hit	name	run	two
bed	except	holiday	near	same	uncle
began	exit	home	new	say	use
big	eyes	horse	night	school	usual
bird	family	hot	nine	see	voice
birthday	far	hour	noise	seven	walk
bit	farm	house	none	shoes	want
black	fast	hurt	north	show	warm
blue	father	ice cream	old	sister	watch
boat	favourite	inside	one	six	water
book	feet	jump	open	sleep	way
box	fell	just	outside	slow	weather
boy	felt	keep	own	small	week
bread	few	kept	park	soon	west
bring	find	kind	party	sound	white
brother	first	knew	pass	south	whole
bus	fish	knife	people	spring	win
busy	five	know	pet	start	window
buy	flew	later	piece	stay	winter
call	floor	left	place	stop	woman
cat	fly	less	plane	story	women
caught	food	let	plant	street	word
city	found	light	play	suddenly	work
cold	four	like	please	summer	world
come	friend	little	plenty	sun	write
cool	front	live	pretty	sure	wrong
dad	full	long	pull	talk	year
day	fun	look	push	take	yellow
dinner	get	lot	put	tell	yesterday
do	girl	love	quickly	ten	
dog	give	lunch	quiet	thing	
doll	go	make	rain	think	
door	great	man	ran	three	
		men			

COMPOUND WORDS

aftershock
anthill
backpack
backside
backyard
bandstand
barnyard
baseball
basketball
bathroom
bedroom
bedtime
blackboard
bookcase
bookend
bookmark
bridegroom
bridesmaid
broomstick
bulldozer
bullfrog
bullseye
buttercup
buttermilk
butterscotch
cardboard
cartwheel
carwash
cornflakes
cowboy
cowshed
daydream
daylight
daytime
dipstick
doorman
doorstep
doorstop
downcast
downhill
downplay
downright
downstage
downstairs
downstream
downtown
drainpipe
driveway
eggplant
eggshell
eyebrow
eyelash
eyeliner
farmland
farmyard
fingernail
firebreak
firelight
fireman
fireplace
fireproof
flashlight
foolhardy
football
footloose
footman
footpath
footprint
footstool
forthright
gemstone
gentleman
goalkeeper
grandfather
grandmother
grandstand
grapefruit
grapevine
greenkeeper
halfback
handbag
handstand
handwork
haystack
headlight
heartfelt
herself
hillside
himself
homeland
homework
horseback
horsehair
horseplay
horseshoe
hosepipe
houseboat
household
hovercraft
icebox
inside
jukebox
junkyard
kickboxing
kitbag
knapsack
knockout
landslide
leadlight
leeway
lifeguard
lifeline
lifesaver
lifetime
lighthouse
lightweight
lunchbox
manhole
manpower
matchbox
matchstick
milkshake
moonlight
moonshine
mothballs
mousetrap
mouthorgan
netball
nickname
nightdress
nightfall
nightlight
notebook
notepaper
nursemaid
ourselves
outside
overalls
overcoat
overleaf
overtime
padlock
paintbrush
passionfruit
pathway
penknife
pickpocket
pigsty
policeman
popcorn
porthole
postcard
postman
powerhouse
quarterback
railroad
railway
rainbow
raincoat
raindrops
runway
saddleback
saddlebag
sandbag
scarecrow
shockproof
shoestring
skylight
slipstream
snakeskin
snowball
snowflake
standstill
snowman
softball
spotlight
springtime
starlight
steamroller
stopwatch
stowaway
sunlight
sunshine
teapot
telltale
thunderstorm
timetable
toothbrush
toothpaste
toothpick
toenail
topside
torchlight
towbar
towtruck
underground
underline
underneath
underplay
underscore
underside
understand
uphill
upstairs
upstage
waistcoat
waterbed
watercolour
watercourse
watercress
waterfall
waterfront
waterhole
watermelon
waterproof
watertight
waterway
waterworks
waxworks
weekday
weekend
wheelchair
whirlwind
whiteboard
windmill
wishbone
witchcraft
workroom
workshop
worldwide
yardstick

HOMOPHONES

ail / ale
air / heir
aisle / I'll / isle
allowed /aloud
alms / arms
altar /alter
arc /ark
aren't / aunt
ascent /assent
ate /eight
awe / oar/ or/ ore
bail / bale
bald / bawled
bare / bear
bark / barque
baron /barren
base / bass
be / bee
beach / beech
bean / been
beau / bow
beer / bier
bell /belle
berry / bury
berth / birth
bight / bite
blew / blue
boar / bore
board / bored
boarder / border
bold / bowled
born / borne
bough / bow
boy / buoy
braid / brayed
braise / brays
brake / break
bread / bred
brews / bruise
bridal / bridle
but / butt
buy / by / bye
cannon / canon
canvas / canvass
capital / capitol
carat / carrot
cast / caste
caw / core / corps
cede / seed
ceiling / sealing
cellar / seller
cent / scent / sent
centred / scented
cents / scents / sense
cereal / serial
cheap / cheep
check / cheque
chews / choose
choral / coral
cite / sight / site
clause / claws
coarse / course
coat / cote
colonel / kernel
council / counsel
creak / creek
crews / cruise
cue / queue
curb / kerb
currant / current
cygnet / signet
days / daze
dear /deer
desert /dessert
dew / due
die / dye
died / dyed
dies / dyes
doe/ dough
draft / draught
draw / drawer
dyeing / dying
earn / urn
ewe / you / yew
ewes / use
eye / I
eyelet / islet
faint / feint
fair/ fare
farther / father
fate / fete
feat / feet
find / fined
fir / fur
flaw / floor
flea / flee
flew / flu / flue
floe / flow
flocks / phlox
flour / flower
for / fore / four
fort / fought
foul / fowl
frays / phrase
freeze / frieze
gait / gate
gamble / gambol
genes / jeans
gild / guild
gnaw / nor
gored / gourd
gorilla / guerrilla
grate / great
grater / greater
groan / grown
guessed / guest
hail / hale
hangar / hanger
hart / heart
heal / heel / he'll
hear / here
heard / herd
hears / here's
hew / hue
higher / hire
him / hymn
ho / hoe
hoard / horde
hoarse / horse
hoes / hose
hole / whole
holy / wholly
hour / our
idle / idol
in / inn
Ireland / island
jam / jamb
key / quay
knave / nave
knead / need
knew / new
knight / night
knot / not
know / no
knows / nose
lacks / lax
lain / lane
laps / lapse
larva / lava
lead / led
leak / leek
lessen / lesson
liar / lyre
licence / license
lieu / loo
lightening / lightning
links / lynx
load / lode
loan / lone
loot / lute

HOMOPHONES Continued

made / maid
mail / male
main / mane
maize / maze
mall / maul
manner / manor
mantel / mantle
mare / mayor
marshal / martial
meat / meet / mete
medal / meddle
metal / mettle
meter / metre
might / mite
mind / mined
miner / minor
missed / mist
moan / mown
moat / mote
mode / mowed
more / moor
morn / mourn
morning / mourning
muscle / mussel
mustard / mustered
nay / neigh
none / nun
ode / owed
one / won
paced / paste
packed / pact
pail / pale
pain / pane
pair / pare / pear
passed / past
patience / patients
paw / poor / pore
peace / piece
peak / peek
peer / pier

pedal / peddle
place / plaice
plain / plane
please / pleas
plum / plumb
pole / poll
practice / practise
praise / prays / preys
pray / prey
presence / presents
principal / principle
prise / prize
profit / prophet
quarts / quartz
rain / rein/ reign
raise / rays
rap / wrap
read / reed
read / red
real / reel
rest / wrest
review / revue
right / rite / write
ring / wring
road / rode
roam / Rome
roe / row
role / roll
root / route
rose/ rows
rote / wrote
rough / ruff
rung / wrung
rye / wry
sail / sale
sauce / source
saw / soar / sore
sawed / soared/ sword
scene / seen

scull / skull
sea / see
seam / seem
seas / sees / seize
sew / so / sow
shear / sheer
shore / sure
side / sighed
sighs / size
slay / sleigh
sold / soled
sole / soul
some / sum
son / sun
sort / sought
staid / stayed
stair / stare
stationary / stationery
steal / steel
step / steppe
stile / style
storey / story
straight / strait
serge / surge
tacked / tact
tacks / tax
tail / tale
tare / tear
taught / taut
taw / tore
tea / tee
team / teem
tear / tier
teas / tease
tense / tents
Thai / tie
their / there / they're
threw / through
throne / thrown
thyme / time

tide / tied
tire / tyre
to / too/ two
toe / tow
told / tolled
tracked / tract
tracks / tracts
troop / troupe
trussed / trust
vain / vane/ vein
vale / veil
vault / volt
wade / weighed
wail / whale
waist/ waste
wait / weight
waive / wave
war / wore
warn /worn
watt/ what
way/ weigh / whey
weak / week
wear / where
weather / whether
weave / we've
which / witch
while / wile
whirled / world
whine / wine
who's / whose
wood / would
yoke / yolk
your / you're

HOMOGRAPHS

Words in red can be pronounced in different ways.

abuse
arms
back
ball
bank
bar
bark
base
bat
bay
beam
bear
beat
bill
bit
blind
block
blow
board
booty
bow
brand
cape
case
cast
change
chop
close
club
coach
coast
coat
cold
column
conduct
corn
count
court
craft
crane
cricket
crop
cross
crow
desert
dock
down
draught
draw
drill
drive
drone
duck
express
fair
fast
felt
file
fill
fine
fire
fit
flag
fleet
float
fold
foot
form
game
gape
grain
grate
grave
ground
gum
hail
hamper
hand
hide
hit
hold
host
iron
jam
jar
joint
jumper
just
kid
kind
kite
lap
last
lay
lead
lean
leaves
left
let
letter
lie
lift
light
line
list
litter
lock
log
mail
march
mass
master
match
may
mean
might
mine
mint
minute
mould
mount
nail
note
object
order
organ
page
palm
pass
patient
peal
plot
plug
pole
port
post
pound
power
private
prune
pupil
race
range
rank
read
record
rent
rest
rifle
right
ring
rock
roll
rose
round
row
ruler
rung
sack
safe
save
scale
scales
seal
season
shed
sheet
sign
sink
smoke
soil
sound
sow
speaker
spell
spoke
spring
squash
staff
stage
stall
stand
star
state
steer
stern
stick
stock
stole
strike
stud
stump
subject
suit
swallow
swift
table
tear
temper
tile
till
top
train
trip
tumbler
turn
vote
wake
watch
wave
well
wind
work
wound

ANTONYMS

above	**below**
after	**before**
awake	**asleep**
black	**white**
bright	**dull**
clean	**dirty**
cold	**hot**
come	**go**
dawn	**dusk**
day	**night**
dear	**cheap**
ebb	**flow**
expensive	**cheap**
far	**near**
fast	**slow**
fat	**thin**
fat	**slim**
fresh	**stale**
friend	**foe /enemy**
full	**empty**
good	**bad**
great	**small**
high	**low**
ill	**well**
in	**out**
kind	**unkind**
late	**early**
life	**death**
light	**dark**
light	**heavy**
little	**big**
long	**short**

love	**hate**
morning	**afternoon**
now	**then**
off	**on**
often	**seldom**
old	**new**
old	**young**
open	**close**
open	**shut**
over	**under**
right	**left**
right	**wrong**
sad	**happy**
sink	**float**
sleep	**wake**
small	**large**
smooth	**rough**
smooth	**coarse**
soft	**loud**
soft	**hard**
sooner	**later**
stand	**sit**
stop	**go**
throw	**catch**
top	**bottom**
ugly	**beautiful**
up	**down**
wet	**dry**
wide	**narrow**
wild	**tame**
win	**lose**
with	without

PREFIXES

a on, in, into, to	**ab** off, away, from	**ad** direction, addition	**after** afterwards	**auto** self
aboard	abduct	adjacent	afterburn	autobiography
about	abhor	adjourn	afterlife	autocrat
adrift	abnormal	adjudicate	aftermath	autocue
afoot	abort	adjust	afternoon	autograph
alight	absent	admire	aftershave	autoharp
along	absolute	admit	aftershock	automatic
aloud	absolve	advance	aftertaste	automaton
among	absorb	advantage	afterthought	automobile
anew	abstain	adversity	afterwards	autopilot
away	abstract	advocate		autosuggestion

anti opposed to, against	**ante** before in space/ time	**arch** first, chief	**bi** two	**bene** well
antibiotic	antebellum	arch fiend	bicentenary	benediction
anticlimax	antecedent	arch rival	bicycle	benedictory
anticlockwise	antechamber	arch villain	biennial	benefactor
antidote	antedate	archangel	bifocal	beneficial
antifreeze	antedote	archbishop	bilateral	beneficiary
antigovernment	antemeridiem	archdeacon	bilingual	benefit
antioxidant	antenatal	archduchess	binoculars	benevolence
antiperspirant	anterior	archduke	biped	benevolent
antiquated	anteroom	arch enemy	biplane	
antisocial		archetype	bisect	

circum round	**co** association, action	**contra** opposite/ opposing	**counter** contrary to	**com** with, jointly
circumference	coagulate	contraband	counteract	combination
circumfluent	coaxial	contrabass	counter-attack	combine
circumlocutory	co-dependence	contraception	counter-balance	combustion
circumnavigate	coerce	contraceptive	counter-intelligence	commence
circumscribe	coexist	contradict	countermand	commiserate
circumspect	cohabit	contralto	counter-offensive	commute
circumstance	cohesive	contravene	counterpart	complacent
circumstantial	coincidence		countersign	complain
circumstantiate	cooperate		countersink	complete
circumvent	coordinate		counterweight	compose
				compute

PREFIXES Continued

con with, jointly, in combination	**dis** away, apart reversing effect	**de** separation, negation, reversal	**di** through. between, across, by	**down** downwards
concentrate	disagree	debrief	digest	downfall
condition	disappear	decay	digress	downgrade
confide	disband	decide	dilate	downhearted
congenial	discard	decompose	dilute	downhill
congratulate	discourage	deduct	dimension	downpipe
connect	discover	delay	direct	downpour
consent	dislocate	depend	divergent	downstairs
consider	disobey	destroy	divert	downstream
converge	displace	determine	divest	downtown
convince	dissolve	develop	divulge	downtrodden

dys difficulty, poor condition	**ex** from, out of, utterly, thoroughly	**e** variant of ex	**en** in, into	**extra** beyond, outside, besides
dyscalculia	excavate	elaborate	enable	extradite
dysentery	exclaim	electric	enchant	extragalactic
dysfunctional	exhale	emerge	encircle	extrajudicial
dysgenic	explain	enormous	encourage	extraneous
dyslexia	explore	eradicate	encroach	extraordinary
dyspepsia	export	erase	enforce	extrapolate
dysphasia	ex-president	erect	engulf	extrasensory
dysphonic	exterminate	evacuate	enlighten	extraterrestrial
dysphoria	external	evaluate	enliven	extraterritorial
dysplasia	extreme	evolve	entreat	extravagant

eu good, well	**epi** near, to, against, above, after, in addition to	**fore** front, ahead of time	**hyper** over -excess, exaggeration	**hypo** under, less, less than
eucalypt	epicentre	foreboding	hype	hypo-activity
Eucharist	epicure	forecast	hyperactive	hypochondriac
euchre	epidemic	forefront	hyperbole	hypocrite
eulogy	epidermis	forego	hypermarket	hypocritical
eunuch	epigram	foreground	hyperphysical	hypodermic
euphonium	epilogue	forehead	hypersensitive	hypoglycaemia
eureka	episode	foreshadow	hypersonic	hypotenuse
eurhythmic	epitaph	foretaste	hyperspace	hypothermia
Europe	epithet	foretell	hypertension	hypothesis
euthanasia	epitome	forewarn	hyperventilate	hypothetical

PREFIXES Continued

in not	inter between	im variant of in-	il variant of in-	mis mistaken, wrong, negation
inaccurate inanimate inappropriate inarticulate incredible inexcusable inexplicable informal invincible invisible	interact interfere interject intermingle international internet interrupt interschool intersect interstate	imbalance immature immeasurable immortal immovable impassable impatient impersonal impossible improbable	illegal illegible illegitimate illicit illiterate illogical ill-timed ill-treat ill-gotten ill-founded	misbehave miscalculate misfortune mishap misjudge misplace mispronounce misrepresent mistrust misuse
over above, beyond	**pre** before, prior to	**pro** for, before, in favour of	**post** behind, after	**para** beyond, near, beside, amiss
overall overbearing overboard overdose overdue overhead overjoyed overlook overrate overtake	precaution precede precooked predict prefabricate prefix prejudge prelude premonition presuppose	probation proceed profound prognosis program progress prohibit prologue promote pronounce	postdate posterity postgraduate posthumous postmeridiem post-mortem postnatal postpone postposition postscript	parachute paradox paragon paragraph parallel paramedic paramount paranormal paraphernalia paraphrase
peri around, about, beyond	**re** back, again, reversal	**retro** backwards in space and time	**semi** half	**se** setting apart, taking away
perilous perimeter peri-natal periodic peripatetic peripheral periphery periphrastic periscope periwinkle	refer regain relate relight remake remit replay restore resume return	retroactive retrocede retrofit retroflex retrograde retrogressive retrorocket retro-rocket retrospect retrospective retroversion	semicircle semicolon semiconscious semi-desert semidetached semi-final semiprecious semiquaver semiskilled semitone	secede secluded secrete secure security seduce select semester sequence severe

PREFIXES Continued

syn association (like co-)	sym variant of syn-	sub under, not quite	super above, superior	tri three
synagogue	symbol	subcontract	supercharged	triangle
synchronise	symbolical	subheading	superimpose	triathlon
syncopate	symmetrical	submerge	superintendent	triceps
syndicate	symmetry	subsonic	supermarket	tricolour
syndrome	sympathise	substandard	supernatural	tricycle
synergy	sympathy	substitute	supersede	triennial
synopsis	symphony	subterranean	superstar	trilogy
syntax	symphystic	subtitle	superstructure	tripartite
synthesis	symposium	subtropical	super-tanker	triplets
synthetic	symptom	subway	supervise	tripod

trans across, beyond	ultra beyond in space and time	un not, opposite to, reversal of state	under below, place or situation	up upwards
transcontinental	ultra sensitive	unarmed	underclothes	update
transfer	ultraconservative	unbeatable	underdog	upgrade
transform	ultracritical	unbend	underestimate	upheaval
translate	ultra-filter	unclean	undergrowth	uphill
translucent	ultraloyal	undesirable	underline	uplifted
transmit	ultramarine	unfold	undermine	upmarket
transparent	ultraradical	untimely	underneath	upright
transport	ultrasonic	untraceable	undernourished	upstage
transpose	ultrasound	untruth	undervalue	upstart
transverse	ultraviolet	unusual	underweight	upstream

ADJECTIVE-FORMING SUFFIXES

al	ive	ish	ic	ent
casual	active	babyish	bombastic	deficient
coastal	attentive	brownish	comic	dependent
lethal	attractive	devilish	domestic	despondent
local	compulsive	foolish	dramatic	efficient
minimal	effective	impish	idiotic	eloquent
occasional	festive	oldish	optimistic	insolent
personal	impulsive	peckish	pessimistic	proficient
regional	negative	Spanish	rustic	prominent
thermal	positive	stylish	static	reverent
usual	sensitive	sweetish	toxic	transient

ful	less	some	able	ible
careful	breathless	awesome	agreeable	admissible
cheerful	defenceless	bothersome	changeable	divisible
colourful	fearless	cumbersome	comfortable	edible
doubtful	leaderless	flavoursome	desirable	horrible
fanciful	merciless	gruesome	fashionable	incredible
helpful	motherless	handsome	miserable	invisible
peaceful	numberless	loathsome	reasonable	possible
powerful	relentless	meddlesome	reliable	responsible
thoughtful	sleepless	tiresome	untraceable	sensible
truthful	timeless	wearisome	workable	terrible

er / est	ial	ous	ious	y
bigger / est	beneficial	adventurous	delicious	busy
calmer / est	commercial	continuous	devious	fizzy
faster / est	differential	fabulous	fallacious	funny
happier / est	essential	famous	gracious	greasy
higher / est	influential	generous	illustrious	greedy
hotter / est	initial	jealous	impervious	grubby
poorer / est	official	momentous	malicious	happy
later / est	partial	mountainous	officious	hungry
longer / est	potential	nervous	precious	lazy
older / est	preferential	ominous	spacious	risky
slower / est	sequential	onerous		rocky
small / est	special	perilous	**ual**	speedy
strong / est	superficial	pompous	continual	sunny
thicker / est	territorial	venomous	usual	tasty
thinner / est	trivial	zealous	visual	tricky
wetter / est				

NOUN-FORMING SUFFIXES

acy	ant	ary /ory /ery	ance	ence
accuracy	assistant	cemetery	abundance	competence
bureaucracy	attendant	diary	accordance	conference
conspiracy	combatant	dispensary	circumstance	correspondence
democracy	commandant	documentary	distance	dependence
fallacy	confidant	eatery	disturbance	eloquence
intimacy	consonant	factory	elegance	experience
legacy	dependant	infirmary	entrance	inference
lunacy	pedant	mortuary	nuisance	innocence
piracy	pendant	refectory	performance	persistence
privacy	servant	seminary	reluctance	pretence

ium	er	ism	ist	ice
aquarium	announcer	communism	dentist	accomplice
auditorium	baker	escapism	egotist	apprentice
conservatorium	builder	fanaticism	exhibitionist	armistice
millennium	buyer	fatalism	extremist	cornice
planetarium	cricketer	favouritism	guitarist	injustice
podium	dancer	idealism	opportunist	novice
premium	driver	impressionism	racist	police
solarium	photographer	racism	sadist	practice
stadium	teacher	rheumatism	soloist	prejudice
terrarium	trader	unionism	violinist	service

cle	hood	itis	ion	tion
debacle	adulthood	appendicitis	apprehension	collection
icicle	babyhood	arthritis	conclusion	competition
manacle	brotherhood	bronchitis	decision	destination
monocle	childhood	dermatitis	derision	education
oracle	falsehood	fibrositis	illusion	pollution
particle	fatherhood	laryngitis	impression	explanation
pinnacle	motherhood	meningitis	occasion	illustration
receptacle	parenthood	peritonitis	opinion	instruction
spectacle	priesthood	sinusitis	pension	invitation
tentacle	sainthood	tonsillitis	question	recreation

MORE NOUN-FORMING SUFFIXES

ment	ness	ship	ity	ian
amazement	awkwardness	censorship	authenticity	electrician
amusement	carelessness	companionship	complicity	guardian
appointment	darkness	craftsmanship	domesticity	Italian
engagement	laziness	fellowship	electricity	mathematician
entertainment	madness	friendship	facility	musician
management	selfishness	horsemanship	familiarity	paediatrician
movement	softness	leadership	mediocrity	pedestrian
predicament	sweetness	partnership	security	politician
refreshment	tenderness	relationship	similarity	technician
wonderment	uneasiness	scholarship	toxicity	vegetarian
age	**ent / ee**	**or**	**ette**	**ar**
blockage	agent	actor	cigarette	beggar
bondage	antecedent	author	dinette	burglar
breakage	devotee	conductor	diskette	bursar
damage	employee	contractor	etiquette	commissionar
foliage	evacuee	doctor	kitchenette	registrar
hostage	precedent	mentor	marionette	scholar
leafage	president	sailor	rosette	scimitar
leakage	refugee	sculptor	silhouette	tartar
postage	respondent	senator	suffragette	vicar
storage	student	visitor	usherette	

ADVERB-FORMING SUFFIXES

ly	ward/s	wise	way/s
busily	afterward	anticlockwise	always
daily	backwards	clockwise	anyway
gladly	downwards	crosswise	away
honestly	forwards	lengthwise	halfway
lately	homeward	likewise	lengthways
presently	inwards	moneywise	longways
quietly	outwards	otherwise	sideways
reluctantly	towards	pennywise	
slowly	wayward	timewise	
usually	westward	waterwise	

VERB-FORMING SUFFIXES

ate	en	ise	fy
excavate	enlighten	advertise	falsify
investigate	flatten	analyse	horrify
irrigate	lengthen	apologise	identify
nominate	open	capitalise	magnify
operate	shorten	criticise	mystify
populate	stiffen	maximise	notify
regulate	straighten	minimise	qualify
separate	strengthen	recognise	signify
tolerate	weaken	synthesise	simplify
ventilate	widen	utilise	terrify
le	**ing**	**ed**	**er**
chuckle	collecting	charmed	chatter
dangle	constructing	demonstrated	flicker
gurgle	delaying	extended	gather
juggle	employing	grounded	muster
meddle	intending	hauled	shudder
sidle	listening	lied	snigger
sparkle	parading	minded	stammer
startle	residing	ploughed	stutter
stumble	shopping	stormed	wander
tremble	towering	teased	wonder

LATIN, GREEK
AND OTHER LANGUAGE ROOTS

ROOT	MEANING	EXAMPLES
ab	from	Aboriginal, absent, abduct, abstract, absolve, abdicate
actus	I act	actor, action, active, react, reaction, reactive, activate
aequus	equal, fair, just	equal, equivalent, equinox, equality, equity, equator, equate
aero	air	aerial, aeroplane, aerodrome, aeronaut, aerobics, aerosol
albus	white	albino, album, albumen, albatross,
alter	other of two	alter, alteration, alternate, alternative, altercation
altus	high	altitude, exalt, altimeter, altocumulus
ambulo	I walk	amble, perambulate, perambulator (pram), somnambulist
amplus	large	ample, amplify, amplitude
angulus	corner	angle, rectangle, triangle, angular
anima	soul, breath, life	animated, inanimate, animal, animation, animalism
annus	a year	annual, anniversary, annuity, biennial, perennial, triennial
aqua	water	aquatic, aquarium, aqua-aerobics, aqua, aquamarine
arbor	tree	arbour, arboreal, arboreous, arboriculture, arboretum
arcticus	northern	Arctica, Antarctica, arctic
arcus	bow	arch, archway, arc, arcade
aster	star	asterisk, asteroid, astronaut, astrology, astronomy, astral
audio	I hear	audience, audiovisual, auditorium, auditory, audible
auster	southern	Australia, Australian
autos	self	autograph, autobiography, automatic, automaton, autocracy
avis	a bird	aviary, aviation, aviator, avionics
baros	weight	barometer, isobar, baritone
bellum	war	rebel, rebellious, rebellion, belligerent, belligerence
biblios	book	bibliography, Bible, bibliophile
bios	life	biography, autobiography, biology
bonus	good	bounty, bountiful, bonus, abound
brevis	short	brief, briefly, brevity, abbreviate, abbreviation
cado / casus	I fall	accident, accidental, casual, decadence, decay, decide, deciduous, incident, occasion
caedo	I cut, kill	incision, incisive, homicide, suicide, genocide, patricide
capio /captus	I take	capture, captivate, captive, accept, anticipate, capable
caput /capitus	the head	capital, capitulate, captain
caro / carnis	flesh	carnivore, carnivorous, carcasss
cavus	hollow	cave, cavern, cavity, excavate, excavation
cedo / cessus	I go	accede, access, antecedent, concession, intercede, recede, precede, precedence, proceed, process, procession, succeed, success, incessant, recess, recession, excess

LATIN, GREEK AND OTHER LANGUAGE ROOTS

ROOT	MEANING	EXAMPLES
censeo census	I judge or value	census, censor, incentive, concentrate
centum	one hundred	century, centenary, centigrade, centipede, centimetre
circum	round	circumnavigate, circumference, circle, circuit, circulate
cirrus	curl	cirrus, cirrocumulus
cito / citatus	I rouse	incite, excite, recite, recitation, citation, resuscitate
civis	a citizen	city, citizen, civic, civil, civilian, civilise, civilisation
clamo	I shout	exclaim, exclamation, proclaim, proclamation, clamour, declaim
clino	I bend	decline, incline, inclination, recline
cogito	I think	cogitate, cognitive, cognition, incognito, recognise
colo / cultus	I till	cultivate, agriculture, colony, colonial, cult, horticulture,
contra	against	contradict, contrary, contraband, contraceptive
cor / cordis	the heart	cordiality, courage, discourage, encourage, concord, record
corpus	the body	corps, in/corporation, in/corporate, in/corpulence, corpse
credo	I believe	credible, incredible, credulity, incredulous, credence, credentials
cresco	I grow	decrease, increase, increment, incremental
crimen	charge	crime, criminal, incrimination, recrimination, discriminate
crux / cruces	cross	crucial, crucify, crucifix, crusade, crux
cumulus	heap	altocumulus, cirrocumulus, accumulate, accumulation
curro cursus	I run	courier, course, current, cursive, cursory, incur, occur
cyclus	wheel	cycle, bicycle, tricycle, cyclic, cylinder, cylindrical
debeo	I owe	debt, debitor, debit, indebted
decem	ten	decade, decimal, December, decimate, decagon, decathlon
demos	the people	democracy, democratic, demonstrate, epidemic, endemic
dens / dentis	tooth	dental, dentist, dentistry, dentures, indent, trident
desertus	waste	desert, deserted, desolate, desolation, isolated
dico / dictus	I say	dictate, dictation, dictator, diction, dictionary, edict, predict, contradict, verdict, predicate, indicate, indication, indict
doceo / doctus	I teach	doctor, indoctrinate, doctrine, doctorate
dormino	I sleep	dormant, dormitory, dormouse
duco / ductus	I lead	conduct, conductor, abduct, educate, education, introduce, reduce, product, productive, induct, induction, induce, deduce
duo	two	duel, duet
ergon	I work	energy, energetic, energise, surgeon, ergonomic
erro	I wander	errand, errant, error, erroneous
ethos	people	ethos, ethnic, ethnicity, ethnographic
facio / factus	I make, do	manufacture, factory, artificial, defect, perfection, sacrifice, magnificent, magnify, effect, feat
fallo / falsus	I deceive	false, falsify, fallible, infallible, fault

LATIN, GREEK AND OTHER LANGUAGE ROOTS

ROOT	MEANING	EXAMPLES
femina	woman	feminine, female, effeminate, effeminacy
fendo	I strike	defend. defence, self-defence
finis	the end	final, finale, finite, infinite, finalise, finance, finish, finality
fircus	treasury	fiscal, confiscate, confiscation
flecto	I bend	reflect, reflection, inflect, inflection, flexible, deflect
fortis	strong	comfort, discomfort, for, enforce, enforcement, forceful, fortify, reinforce, fortify, fortification
frango	I break	fraction, fragile, fracture, infraction
frater	brother	fraternity, fratricide, fraternise
frigus	cold	frigid, refrigerate, refrigerator
fugio	I flee	fugitive, refuge, refugee
fundo fusus	I pour	funnel, fund, refund, foundry, refuse
gamos	marriage	bigamist, bigamy, monogamist, monogamy
geo	earth	geography, geocentric, geometry, geology, geomagnetic, geophysics, geothermic, geostatic, geochronology
gradus	step	grade, gradient, degrade, gradual, progress, regress, retrograde, retrogressive
grapho	I write	graph, graphic, autograph, biography, autobiography, geography, homograph, monograph, paragraph, lithograph, telegraph, topography, photograph, phonograph
habito	I dwell	habitat, habitation, inhabit, uninhabitable, habit, habitual
homo / hominus	man	homage, homicide, homo sapiens, human, humane, hobo
horreo	I shudder	horrid, horrible, horrify, horrific, abhor, abhorrence
hospes	guest	hospital, hospice, hospitable, host, hostess
impero	I command	emperor, imperial, empire
insula	island	insular, insulate, peninsula
integer	whole	integer, integral, integrity
jacio jactus	I throw	eject, reject, conjecture, inject, project, subject, interject
judex	judge	judge, judgemental, judgement, judicial, judicious, prejudice, adjudicate, adjudicator, adjust, adjustment, readjust
jungo / junctus	I join	conjunction, junction, injunction
juro	I swear	jury, perjury
justus	fitting, right	just, unjust, justice, injustice, justify, justly, justification
juvenis	young	juvenile
kilo	one thousand	kilogram, kilometre, kilowatt
latus laterus	side	lateral, latitude, equilateral, unilateral, multilateral
lego / lectus	read, gather, choose	collect, recollect, dialect, elect, elegant, eligible, elite, legible, illegible, lectern, lecture, legend, neglect, college
liber	free	liberate, liberal, liberty, deliberate, Libra

LATIN, GREEK AND OTHER LANGUAGE ROOTS

ROOT	MEANING	EXAMPLES
locus	place	locality, local, locate, dislocate, location, locomotive
loquor	I speak	eloquent, eloquence, elocution, loquacious
lumen	light	illuminate, luminous
luna	moon	lunar, lunatic
magnus	great	magnitude, magnificent, magnate, main, magnify, magnanimous
manus	hand	manual, manacle, manage, manipulate, manuscript, manufacture
mater	mother	maternal, maternity, matriarch
memor	mindful	memento, memoirs, memorable, memory, remember, reminisce
mens / mentis	mind	mental, mentality, mention, mentor, demented, human, woman
metior / mensus	I measure	immense, metre, mete
metron	measure	barometer, chronometer, diameter, perimeter, gasometer, micrometer, symmetry, asymmetric
migro	I wander	migrate, migrant, immigrant, immigration, emigrate, emigration, migratory, transmigrate
micros	very small	microbe, microscope, microfiche, microcosm
minor	small	minus, minimum, minority, minute, miniscule
mito / missus	I send	transmit, transmitter, emit, missile
mors	death	mortal, mortally, mortality, mortuary, immortal, mortgage
multus	many	multiply, multitude
muto	I change	commute, mutate, mutation, mutual
natus	I am born	nature, natural, unnatural, innate, native, nativity, natal
navis	ship	naval, navy, nave, navigate, navigation
nomen	name	name, nominate, numeral, enumerate, numerator, nominal
octo	eight	octagon, octagonal, octopus, octave, octogenarian, October
oculaus	eye	ocular, oculist, binoculars
omnis	all	omnibus, omnipotent, omnivore, omnivorous
opto	I desire	option, optional, adopt, adoption, opt
orbis	circle	orbit, exorbitant
origine	beginning	originate, original, aborigine, aboriginal
ovum	egg	oval, ovate, ovum, ovary, ovarian
paleo	old, ancient	palaeontology, palaeontologist, palaeography, Palaeolithic
pars / partis	part	department, departmental, compartment, apartment, partial, particle, separate, partition
pater	father	paternal, patricide, patriarch, patriarchal
pathos	feeling	pathology, pathetic, sympathy, empathy, pathos
pectus	breast	pectoral, expectorate, expectoration
pello	I drive	propel, propeller, compel, compulsion, expel, expulsion, impel
peri	around	perimeter, periscope, periphery, peripheral

LATIN, GREEK AND OTHER LANGUAGE ROOTS

ROOT	MEANING	EXAMPLES
pes / pedis	the foot	centipede, impede, impediment, pedestrian. pedal, pedestal
phono	voice, sound	phone, phonic, gramophone, megaphone, earphones, symphony
phos	light	phosphorous, photograph, photosynthesis
plus / pluris	more	plus, plural, surplus
polis	people	police, politics, politician, political
poly	many	polygamy, polygon, Polynesia, monopoly
pono / positus	I place	deposit, compose, compositor, pose, position, imposition, propound, oppose, opposite, opponent, interpose, expose, depose, repose, transpose
populus	the people	populate, population, popular, public, publican, publish, republic
porto	I carry	portable, export, import, important, transport, report, reporter, support
pous podus	foot	podiatrist, podiatry, podium, tripod
primus	first	prime, primary, primitive, primal
qualis	of which kind	qualify, disqualify, quality
quantus	how much	quantity, quantify
radius	ray	radius, radial, radiate, irradiate
repellere	drive back	repel, repellent, repulse, repulsive
repo	I creep	reptile, surreptitious
rex / regis	king	regent, regal, reign
rota	wheel	rotate, rotor, rotary, rotation
rumpo / ruptus	I break	rupture. erupt, eruption, abrupt, interrupt, irruption
sal	salt	salad, salt, salty, salary, sauce, sausage
scando	I climb	ascend, ascent, descend, descent, ascension
sciential	I know	conscience, conscious, unconscious, consciousness, science, scientist, scientific, omniscient
scribo	I write	scribe, script, describe, description, inscribe, inscription, prescribe, prescription, conscript, ascribe, scribble
seco / sectus	I cut	dissect, section, sect, sector, segment, secateurs
sedeo / sessus	I sit	sedentary, sediment, session
senex	old man	senior, senile, senate, senator
sentio	I feel	assent, consent, dissent, sense, nonsense, resent, resentful, sensible, sensitive, sentiment, sentimental
servo	I keep	preserve, preservative, preservation, conserve, reserve, serve, servant, servile
signum	sign	sign, signal, signature, signify, significant, resign, consign
skopeo	I see	periscope, microscope, telescope, scope

LATIN, GREEK AND OTHER LANGUAGE ROOTS

ROOT	MEANING	EXAMPLES
sol	sun	solar, solstice
solus	alone	solitude, solace, solitary, desolate, isolated, solo, soloist
solve	loosen	dissolve, dissolution, solve, resolve, solvent
specio	I see	spectacle, spectacles, inspect, respect, specimen, spectacular
spiro	I breathe	transpire, expire, aspire, aspiration, respiration, spirit, spiritual, dispirited
sto	I stand	constant, obstacle, stagnant, station, stationary, statue, stature, status, statuesque
struo / structus	I build	construct, instruct, obstruct, destruction, restructure
tango / tactus	I touch	tactile, tag, contagious, tact, tactful, tactless, intact, contact
tele	afar	television, telephone, telecast, telegraph, telepathy, telescope
tempus	time	temporary, contemporary, extemporary, temporal
tendo / tensus	I stretch	tense, tension, attend, contend, distend, extend, intend, pretend, intense, superintendent, tend, tendency, tender
teneo	I hold	tenet, contain, continent, abstain, continue, sustain, detain, obtain, retain, certain, tenacious, tenant
terra	earth	terrace, terracotta, terra firma, territory, territorial, terrarium, terrain, terrier, Terra Australis
therme	heat	isotherm, thermometer, thermal
testis	witness	test, testify, testimony, testament, testimonial
Traho / tractus	I draw	attract, betray, distract, contract, detract, portrait, portray, retrace, retract, subtract, trace, traction, tractor, protractor, subcontract
unus	one	unit, unify, union, unite, university, unity, unison, uniform, universal, reunion, commune, community
verto / versus	I turn	advertise, converse, conversation, reverse, reversal, revert, invert, convert
verus	true	verdict, verify, verily, very
video / visus	I see	vision, visual, evidence, provide, video, visualise, television, provision, videotape, visible, invisible, revise, revision, advise
vinco	I conquer	invincible, convince, victim, victor, victory, victorious
voco	I call	vocal, vocalise, vocation, irrevocable, advocate
vorare	to devour	carnivore, carnivorous, herbivore, herbivorous, omnivore, omnivorous, voracious
zoon	an animal	zoo, zoology, zoologist, zodiac,

GLOSSARY

abbreviation	Word made short by leaving letters out. ***kg** kilogram; **Mr** Mister; **pm** post meridiem*
acronym	Type of abbreviation formed from the first letters of other words. ***Anzac** Australian and New Zealand Army Corps*
adjective	Word used to describe a person, place or thing. ***hot** coffee; **tall** tree; **old** friend*
adverb	Word that adds to the meaning of the verb. It tells us how, when, where and for how long something is happening. *I moved house **yesterday**. She moved **quickly**. Put it **here** on the table. She trains **weekly**.*
alphabet	A series of symbols we call letters. We use these letters to represent speech sounds to compose written language.
antonyms	Words opposite in meaning to each other. *hot, cold; long, short; happy, unhappy*
apostrophe	A punctuation mark (') which shows: 1. ownership. *Chad's book; butterflies' wings* 2. where letters have been left out in contractions. *e'er, can't, didn't, it's*
articles **- definite** **- indefinite**	Short words that introduce a noun or noun group. ***The** cabbage. **A** boy. **An** hour.* The word *the*. Used when subject is known by the reader. ***The** prime minister.* The words *a* and *an. An* is used before a word beginning with a vowel. ***An** orange.*
base word	A word from which others are built. ***rest**ing; **rest**ed; **rest**ful; **rest**less; un**rest***
capital letters	Upper case letters used at the beginning of a sentence, for proper nouns (names) and in acronyms. ***G**ive the ball to **J**acob. **W**e will watch the **O**lympic **G**ames on **TV**.*
common endings	Letters most often added to the ends of words. *–ing, -s, -es, -er, -est, -y, -ly*
compound word	Two words joined together. *sea + horse = seahorse; home + sick = homesick*
conjunctions	Words that join ideas together in a meaningful way. *Jack **and** Jill. It's getting dark, **so** I'll turn on the light. He was late **because** he lost his way. Wait **until** I call you.*
consonants	21 of the 26 letters of the alphabet that represent speech sounds. *b c d f g h j k l m n p q r s t v w x y z*
consonant blends	2 consonants that together make a blended sound. *bl*ack; *sl*ide; *fr*og; *pl*ay
consonant 'buddies' **- th** **- ch**	2 consonants together that represent one speech sound. *sh, ch, th, wh, ph* Can be voiced (***th**em, **th**is, **th**at*) or unvoiced (***th**ink, **th**ick, ba**th***) Can be 'hard' (***Ch**ristmas, **ch**oir, an**ch**or*) or 'soft' (***ch**ef, **ch**andelier, para**ch**ute*)
contraction	Shortened word or words. *ever — e'er; can not — can't; it is — it's* An apostrophe marks the missing letters.
dictionary	A book of words and meanings arranged in alphabetical order: A — Z.

high frequency words	Words that occur most often in speaking, writing and reading. *do come was have what saw*
homonyms	Words that are said or spelled the same, but have different meanings.
homographs	Words that are spelt the same with different meanings. ***Ring** me! I lost my **ring**.* Some homographs can be pronounced differently. ***Bow** before your king. He fought with **bow** and arrows.*
homophones	Words that sound the same, but have different spelling. *tail, tale; for, four; know, no; to, too, two; horse, hoarse*
Latin/Greek roots	The basis on which many words in English have been built. *verto—I turn: vertical, reverse, reversible, invert, inverse, converse, convertible*
letters **- letter q** **- letter c** **- letter g**	Symbols used to write words. They represent the sounds of spoken words. This letter is always followed by 'u': *queen, quiet, quickly, quit* Represents two sounds: 'hard' *car, cup, coat*; and 'soft' *city, cent, cycle* Represents two sounds: 'hard' *girl, go, game*; and 'soft' *gym, page, gist*
nouns **- common** **- proper**	Words that name people, animals, places and things. *man, mouse, park, cup* The names of everyday things around us. *chair, food, house, shop, tree* The given names of people, places and special events. *Joel, Darwin, Australia Day, April*
object	Person or thing affected by the action of the verb, either directly (*I drank the **milk***) or indirectly (*I gave **him** a book*).
participle (present)	Word formed by adding *–ing* to the base verb. Used to show continuous action (*I was **walking***); as verbal adjective (***walking** stick*); as verbal noun (***Swimming** is good exercise*) and to begin phrases (***Standing** on tip-toe, I could see …*).
participle (past)	Word generally formed by adding *–ed* to the base verb. Used with a helping verb to show past tense (*I had **walked** home*); as verbal adjective (***potted** plants*) and to begin phrases. (*The floods, **viewed** from the helicopter, **spread out over** the entire countryside*.) Some have an irregular form. *drive, driven; fly, flown; draw, drawn*)
plural	Numbers more than one thing. Applied to nouns, pronouns and verbs. Plural nouns are formed by adding *–s* or *–es* to the singular noun. *cars, buses, peaches, boxes, cakes.* Some plural nouns are irregular *child, children; mouse, mice.*
prefix	A syllable attached to the beginning of a word to change its meaning. *like, **dis**like; regular, **ir**regular; plane, **bi**plane; warn, **fore**warn*
pronoun **- personal** (singular) **- personal** (plural) **- possessive** (singular) **- possessive** (plural) **- subject position** **- object position** **- relative**	Word standing in place of a noun. They have singular, plural and possessive forms. *I, me, you, he, him, she, her, it* *we, us, you, they, them* *my, mine, your, yours, his, her, hers, its* *our, ours, your, yours, their, theirs* *I, you, he, she, it, we, they* *me, you, him, her, us, them* Word used instead of a noun to connect one clause with another. These pronouns are *who, whom* (of people), *which, that* (of things).
preposition	Word used to position people and things. They often begin (prepositional) phrases. ***in** the park; **at** the movies; **under** the chair.*

proofreading	Checking for errors in written text.
phrase	A group of words that add detail to sentences. They have no subject nor verb, so can only make sense within a sentence. *The man **in the straw hat** caught a fish.*
rhyming words	Words that end in the same letter string (visual rhyme) *cat, hat, sat, flat, chat;* or the same sound (auditory rhyme) *pair, bear, fare, heir*.
schwa sound	Sound most often used in spoken English. It appears in unstressed syllables. It can be written in different ways – *about; sister; delicious; conversation.* The sound is rather unclear, like a small grunt. To spell words with schwa sounds, you need to remember what the words **look** like.
silent letters	Letters in written words that are not sounded when spoken. The *k* in *know;* the *w* in *write;* the *b* in *lamb.*
singular	Numbers one thing. Applied to nouns, pronouns and verbs. *plane, it, eats*
spelling rules	Some general tips to aid correct spelling. There are always exceptions to the rules.
suffix	A syllable attached to the end of a word to change the way the word is used. *care — care**ful*** (adjective), *care**less*** (adjective), *careless**ly*** (adverb)
subject	Who or what a sentence is about. ***A lazy wind** stirred the leaves.*
subject /verb agreement	Subject and verb need always to agree in number. A singular subject has a singular verb. *The horse is eating oats.* A plural subject has a plural verb. *The horses are eating oats.*
syllable	When we say a word, a syllable is one 'chunk' of sound (or one mouth movement). *box* (1) *de/lay* (2) *com/pan/y* (3) *sat/is/fy/ing* (4)
tense	Shows when events are happening: *are happening now* (present time); *have already happened* (past time) or *will happen* (future time). To show tense, we alter the verb. We can change the verb (*swim swam swum*); we can add *-s,-ed* (*jump jumps jumped*); use a helping verb (*will visit; shall see)* or use a helping verb with a participle (*is running; was skipping; have watched; had sailed*).
verb **verb helpers**	One or more words that tell us what is 'going on' in a sentence. *Jack **is picking** grapes. Ella **reads** books. Tom **rode** his bike to school.* *He **congratulated** the athlete.* Words that are used in front of the verb to show future tense; (I ***will*** *wait for you.*) or in front of present and past participles. (*We **have** finished eating. They **are** waiting for a bus. She **has** written a book. I **was** not peeping!*) Helpers are called *auxiliary verbs.*
visual pattern	Letter strings that look the same, but may not be pronounced the same. *cough, through, dough, bought* To learn these words, we need to memorise the pattern.
vowels	5 of the 26 letters of the alphabet. *a e i o u* The letter *y* sometimes does the work of the vowels, *e* and *i*.
vowel teams	Vowels working with each other in pairs, or with another consonant to represent different speech sounds. *rain, boat, cow, star, beach, turn...*

TRY THIS

SELECTED ANSWERS

Page

9 Consonants

h r s
p t n

Missing consonants

J p ll
f l w
d k n
d t t

11 Initial consonant blends

r, l, l, l, l, k, r, r, r, r, t, w.

12 Final consonant blends

ramp, mend, wink, hold, crust
stamp, trend, drink, sold, trust.

15 How many vowels are in this text?

a — 21
e — 37
i — 17
o — 17
u — 9

16 Short vowels

a	e	i	o	u
crab	bed	zip	doll	sun
hat	shell	pig	frog	drum
bug	web	chick	dog	cup

17 Short vowels (cont'd)

rat	tap	box	lid	truck
pig	jug	nest	dog	clock
tent	gift	duck	flag	net

Little Red Riding Hook

a,e,u,a,a,i,o,i.
e,i,o,o,e,i,e,i.

18 Long Vowels

face, bike, wave, hose
hive, bone, gate, dive
stove, glue, pie, rake
rose, plate, kite, nose.

35 Stressed syllables

children Saturday basket
reporter tiger volcano
China container doctor
holiday tadpole troublesome
explore jaguar above

43 Verbs

Kara walks to school with Jess, but Jake rides his bike.
Jeff is reading a book and I am doing maths.
When the bell rings, the teacher tells us to go out to lunch.

44 Past tense verbs

dusted	plugged	shopped
packed	limped	buzzed
raced	crossed	played
blinked	hurried	sliced
carried	tricked	ended

44 Irregular past tense verbs

grew	caught
rode	flew
fought	threw
ate	met
stole	made
drank	bought
took	fed

45 Doubling

trap	trapping	trapped	strong	stronger	strongest
hiss	hissing	hissed	fat	fatter	fattest
drag	dragging	dragged	rich	richer	richest
pat	patting	patted	thin	thinner	thinnest
lick	licking	licked	hot	hotter	hottest

46 Words ending in 'e'

baking	liked	slimy
lonely	tribal	statement
tuneful	homeless	shaking
shady	smiled	tubes
placing	wisely	voted

alone amusing singer used spicy

47 Words ending in 'y'

bodies	monkeys
chimneys	bunnies
fairies	trays
holidays	melodies
stories	donkeys
countries	keys

pays	spies
cries	enjoys
buys	prays
tries	flies
stays	employs

48 Word ending in 'f'

shelves	hooves
roofs	knives
chiefs	reefs
calves	beliefs
giraffes	wolves
selves	lives

strive prove
grieve live
save believe

49 'i' before 'e' except after 'c'

grief	achieve	receive	deceive
believe	receipt	hygiene	niece
fierce	besiege	deceit	pier
brief	ceiling	relief	chief

50 Plural nouns

candles	dishes	dancers	apples
beaches	combs	matches	leashes
dresses	stones	crosses	faxes
gases	cups	robots	trumpets

51 Regular and irregular plurals

children men
mice teeth
women feet

52 Plural verbs

likes like
swims swim
plants plant
rides ride

54 Pronouns

2nd person Will <u>you</u> take your dog for a walk?
3rd person <u>They</u> left yesterday to visit their uncle.
1st person <u>We</u> wanted them to come with us.
2nd person <u>You</u> must learn your spelling.
1st person <u>I</u> waited but the bus did not arrive.

56 The Apostrophe

farmer's
James'
kangaroos'
riders'
John's
girls'
ants'
dragonflies'
bike's

57 Contractions

wouldn't
haven't
We'd
couldn't

59 Homynyms

match
duck
watch
left

60 Homographs

present
bow
row
read
house

61 Homophones

grate
sale
heel, sore
bare
site
pear
prey
tale

62 Antonyms

disappear dislocate unclean
untie misjudge disallow
displace untrue misuse
unusual misunderstand disagree
unread disobey mislead

64 Suffixes

impression business
service education
foolish familiarise
reliable tiresome
appointment racist
security socialise
nervous amusement
partnership performance

66 Abbreviations

QLD – Queensland; mL – millilitre; Dr – doctor;
fax – facsimile; kg – kilogram
croc – crocodiles; DVD – digital video disc;
min – minute; Apr – April, c – cent
Uni – University; km – kilometer; limo – limousine;
ff – fortissimo; VIP – very important person
GB – gigabyte; hr – hour; SA – South Australia;
kj – kilojoule, CU – see you.

67 Proofreading

1. fountain 2. splashed
3. white 4. watched
5. reflection 6. quite
7. could 8. drowsily